PIC Microcontroller
Project Book

PIC Microcontroller Project Book

John Iovine

McGraw-Hill

New York   San Francisco   Washington, D.C.   Auckland   Bogotá
Caracas   Lisbon   London   Madrid   Mexico City   Milan
Montreal   New Delhi   San Juan   Singapore
Sydney   Tokyo   Toronto

Cataloging-in-Publication Data is on file with the Library of Congress

McGraw-Hill

A Division of The McGraw·Hill Companies

Copyright © 2000 by The McGraw-Hill Companies, Inc. Printed in the United States of America. Except as permitted under the United States Copyright Act of 1976, no part of this publication may be reproduced or distributed in any form or by any means, or stored in a data base or retrieval system, without the prior written permission of the publisher.

5 6 7 8 9 0 DOC/DOC 0 9 8 7 6 5 4 3 2 1

ISBN 0-07-135479-4

The sponsoring editor of this book was Scott Grillo. The editing supervisor was Steven Melvin, and the production supervisor was Pamela Pelton. It was set in New Century Schoolbook per the MHT design by Michele Pridmore of McGraw-Hill's Professional Book Group composition unit, Hightstown, New Jersey.

Printed and bound by R.R. Donnelley & Sons Company.

McGraw-Hill books are available at special quantity discounts to use as premiums and sales promotions, or for use in corporate training programs. For more information, please write to the Director of Special Sales, Professional Publishing, McGraw-Hill, Two Penn Plaza, New York, NY 10121-2298. Or contact your local bookstore.

 This book is printed on recycled, acid-free paper containing a minimum of 50% recycled de-inked fiber.

Contents

Preface

I know you are interested in programming and using PIC microcontrollers. If not, you would not have picked up this book and be reading this preface. The first question one usually asks when choosing one book over another is, "Which book offers me something more?" Since everyone is looking for something a little different in a book, I can't address anything specific, but to help you make your decision I can state what I feel are the highlights of this book.

Programming

The PICBasic compiler used throughout this book allows ease of using Basic language coupled with the speed of assembly language. Basic is a user-friendly language, it is easier to learn and master than either assembly or C language. When the basic code is compiled to its assembly language equivalents, it is 20 to 100 times faster than standard Basic code, effectively countering the speed advantages C or assembly languages typically offer. The compiled Basic code (assembly language equivalent) is programmed into the PIC microcontroller. As stated, this methodology increases the code execution 20 to 100 times faster than the equivalent interpreted Basic code that is used in other microcontroller systems like the Basic Stamp™.

Cost Savings

Being able to program PIC microcontroller chips directly reduces the overall cost of implementing microcontroller control to a fraction of the cost of other systems. In addition, circuit complexity is also minimized.

Starting at the Beginning

In terms of programming, this book starts at the ground level. Beginning with installing the needed softrware onto your computer's hard drive and proceeding on from there. We begin with a simple project that blinks two LEDs on and off and build more interesting and sophisticated projects out from there.

PIC Microcontroller
Project Book

Microcontroller

What Is a Microcontroller?

A microcontroller is an inexpensive single-chip computer. *Single-chip computer* means that the entire computer system lies within the confines of the integrated circuit chip. The microcontroller on the encapsulated sliver of silicon has features similar to those of our standard personal computer. Primarily, the microcontroller is capable of storing and running a program (its most important feature). The microcontroller contains a CPU (central processing unit), RAM (random-access memory), ROM (read-only memory), I/O (input/output) lines, serial and parallel ports, timers, and sometimes other built-in peripherals such as A/D (analog-to-digital) and D/A (digital-to-analog) converters.

Why Use a Microcontroller?

Microcontrollers, as stated, are inexpensive computers. The microcontroller's ability to store and run unique programs makes it extremely versatile. For instance, one can program a microcontroller to make decisions (perform functions) based on predetermined situations (I/O-line logic) and selections. The microcontroller's ability to perform math and logic functions allows it to mimic sophisticated logic and electronic circuits.

Other programs can make the microcontroller behave like a neural circuit and/or a fuzzy-logic controller. Microcontrollers are responsible for the "intelligence" in most smart devices on the consumer market.

The Future of Electronics Is Here—It's Microcontrollers

Look in any hobbyist electronics magazine from this country or any other. You will see articles that feature the use of microcontrollers, either directly or embedded in the circuit's design. Because of their versatility, microcontrollers add a lot of power, control, and options at little cost. It therefore becomes essential that the electronics engineer or hobbyist learn to program these microcontrollers to maintain a level of competence and to gain the advantages microcontrollers provide in his or her own circuit designs.

If you examine consumer electronics, you will find microcontrollers embedded in just about everything. This is another reason to become familiar with microcontrollers.

Designer Computers

There is a large variety of microcontrollers on the market today. We will focus on a few versatile microcontroller chips called PIC chips (or PICMicro chips) from Microchip Technology.

The PIC Chip

Microchip Technology's series of microcontrollers is called PIC chips. Microchip secured a trademark for the name PIC. Microchip uses PIC to describe its series of PIC microcontrollers. PIC is generally *assumed* to mean programmable interface controller.

Better Than Any Stamp

Parallax Company sells an easy-to-use series of microcontroller circuits called the Basic Stamp. Parallax's Basic Stamps (BS1 and BS2) use Microchip Technology's PIC microcontrollers. What makes the Stamps so popular and easy to use is that they are programmed using a simplified form of the Basic language. Basic-language programming is easy to learn and use. This was the Stamps' main advantage over other microcontroller systems, which have a much longer learning curve because they force their users and developers to learn a niche assembly language. (A niche assembly language is one that is specific to that company's microcontroller and no one else's.)

The Basic Stamp has become one of the most popular microcontrollers in use today. Again, the Basic Stamp's popularity (this bears repeating) is due to its easy-to-learn and easy-to-use Basic-language programming. The PIC's Basic-language system is just as easy to learn and use, and the PIC has enormous benefits that make it better than any Stamp.

The Basic language of the PICBasic compiler that we will use to program the PIC chips is similar to that used in the Basic Stamp series. Programming PIC chips directly has just become as easy as programming Stamps. Now you can enjoy the same easy language the Basic Stamp offers, plus two more very important benefits.

Benefit one: faster speed

Our programmed PIC chips will run their program much faster. If we enter the identical Basic program into a Basic Stamp and into a PIC chip, the programmed PIC chip will run 20 to 100 times faster (depending upon the instructions used) than the Basic Stamp. Here's why.

The BS1 and BS2 Basic Stamp systems use a serial EEPROM memory connected to the PIC chip to store their programs. The basic commands in the program are stored as basic tokens. Basic tokens are like a shorthand for basic commands. When running the program, the Basic Stamp reads each instruction (token and data/address) over the serial line from the external EEPROM memory, interprets the token (converts token to the ML equivalent the PIC can understand), performs the instruction, reads the next instruction, and so on. Each and every instruction goes through these serial load, read, interpret, then perform steps as the program runs. The serial interface reading routine eats up gobs of the microcontroller's CPU time.

In contrast to this operation, when a PIC chip is programmed using the Basic compiler, the Basic program is first converted to a PIC machine-language (hex file) program. The ML program is then uploaded into the PIC chip. Being the native language of the PIC, this machine-language (ML) code does not need to be stored as tokens and interpreted as it runs because the program is written in the PIC chip's native language.

When the PIC chip runs the program, it reads the ML program instructions directly from its on-board memory and performs the instruction. There is no serial interface to an external EEPROM to eat up CPU time. The ML instructions are read in parallel, not bit by bit as in the serial interface. The ML instructions read directly without any basic-token-to-ML-equivalent conversion required. This enables programmed PIC chips to run their code 20 to 100 times faster than the same Basic program code in a Basic Stamp.

Benefit two: much lower cost

The next factor is cost. Using PIC chips directly will save you 75 percent of the cost of a comparable Basic Stamp. The retail price for the BS1, which has 256 bytes of programmable memory, is $34.95. The retail price for the BS2, which has 2K of programmable memory, is $49.95. The 16F84 PIC microcontroller featured throughout this book is more closely comparable to the BS2 Stamp. The 16F84 PIC chip we are using has 1K of programmable memory.

The retail cost of the 16F84 PIC chip is $6.95. To this, add the cost of a timing crystal, a few capacitors, a few resistors, and a 7805 voltage regulator to make a circuit equivalent to that of the Stamp. These components increase the total cost to about $10.00—still well below one-quarter the cost (75 percent savings) currently quoted for the BS2.

And this $10.00 cost for the PIC may be cut substantially in some situations. The PIC 16F84 is an expensive microcontroller with rewritable (flash) memory. If, for instance, you design a circuit (or product) for manufacture that doesn't need to be reprogrammed after it is initially programmed, you can use a one-time programmable (OTP) PIC microcontroller and save about $2.00 to $3.00 on the PIC microcontroller as compared to the cost of a PIC microcontroller with flash (rewritable memory).

In any case, anyone who uses more than a few Stamps a year will find it well worth the investment to completely scrap the Basic Stamp system and jump onto this faster and cheaper microcontroller bandwagon.

If you are an experimenter, developer, or manufacturer or plan to become one, the cost savings are too substantial to consider investing in any other system.

Extra bonus advantage

The footprint of the 16F84 PIC microcontroller chip embedded in another circuit is smaller than the equivalent BS2 Stamp because the Stamps use an external serial EEPROM for memory. While the BS2 may, at first glance, look smaller since it is contained in a 28-pin DIP package, it is not. You can also purchase the 16F84 in surface-mount form and the resulting circuit will have a smaller footprint.

PIC Programming Overview

Programming PIC microcontrollers is a simple three-step process. There's an old saying that there's more than one way to skin a cat, and the same can be said about programming PIC microcontrollers. When you look at the market, you will discover a variety of programmers and compilers for PIC microcontrollers. We will not do a comparison of the products on the market. Instead, we will focus on what we have found to be an easy-to-learn and very powerful Basic-language compiler and its associated programmer board.

Remember, this is an overview. Exact step-by-step instructions are given in the next chapter, when we program a PIC with our first test program.

What to buy

You need to purchase at least three items to start programming and building projects: the PICBasic compiler program, the EPIC programmer (a programming carrier board), and the PIC chip itself. I recommend beginning with the 16F84 PIC microcontroller because it has exactly 1K × 14 of rewritable memory. This memory allows you to reuse the PIC chip many times to test and debug your programs.

The PICBasic compiler (see Fig. 1.1) runs on a standard PC. The program may be run in DOS or in an "MS-DOS prompt" window in the Windows environment. From here on out, the MS-DOS prompt window will be referred to simply as a DOS window. The DOS program will run on everything from an XT-class PC running DOS 3.3 and higher. The program supports a large variety of PIC microcontrollers. The compiler generates ML hex code that may be used with other programming carrier boards. The cost for PICBasic compiler software is $99.95.

Figure 1.1 PICBasic compiler program and manual.

There is a more expensive compiler called the PICBasic Pro that retails for $249.95. Do not purchase this compiler! The PICBasic Pro handles the Peek and Poke commands differently than the standard PICBasic Compiler. So remember to purchase the standard PICBasic Compiler for $99.95.

The EPIC programming carrier board (see Fig. 1.2) has a socket for inserting the PIC chip and connecting it to the computer, via the printer port, for programming. The programming board connects to the computer's printer port (parallel port) using a DB25 cable. If the computer has only one printer port and there is a printer connected to it, the printer must be temporarily disconnected when PIC chips are being programmed. Like the PICBasic compiler, the EPIC programming carrier board supports a wide variety of PIC microcontrollers. The cost for the EPIC programming board with EPIC programming diskette is $59.00. Those who wish to build their own board may purchase a bare PC board with program diskette for $34.95.

The PIC 16F84 pinout is shown in Fig. 1.3. It is a versatile microcontroller with flash memory. Flash memory is a term used to describe this type of

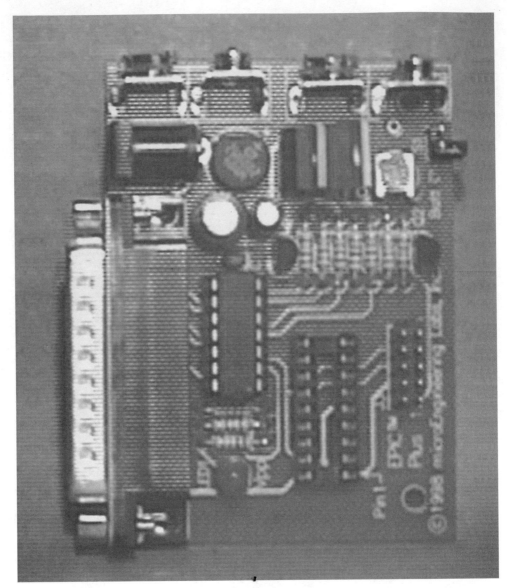

Figure 1.2 EPIC programming carrier board and software.

rewritable memory. The on-board flash memory can endure a minimum of 1000 erase/write cycles, so you can reprogram and reuse the PIC chip at least 1000 times. The program retention time, between erase/write cycles, is approximately 40 years. The 18-pin chip devotes 13 pins to I/O. Each pin may be programmed individually for input or output. The pin status (I/O direction control) may be changed on the fly via programming. Other features include power on reset, power-saving sleep mode, power-up timer, and code protection,

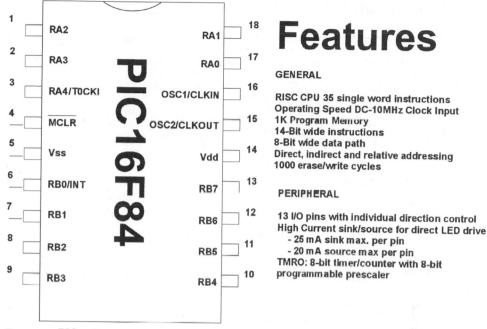

Figure 1.3 PIC 16F84 pinout.

Features

GENERAL

RISC CPU 35 single word instructions
Operating Speed DC-10MHz Clock Input
1K Program Memory
14-Bit wide instructions
8-Bit wide data path
Direct, indirect and relative addressing
1000 erase/write cycles

PERIPHERAL

13 I/O pins with individual direction control
High Current sink/source for direct LED drive
  - 25 mA sink max. per pin
  - 20 mA source max per pin
TMRO: 8-bit timer/counter with 8-bit
programmable prescaler

among others. Additional features and architecture details of the PIC 16F84 will be given as we continue.

Step 1: Writing the Basic-language program

PICBasic programs are written using a word processor. Any word processor that is able to save its text file as ASCII or DOS text may be used. Just about every commercial word processor available has this option. Use the Save as command and choose MS-DOS text, DOS text, or ASCII text. The text file you write with the word processor will be compiled into a program. If you don't own a word processor, you can use Windows Notepad, which is included with Windows 3.X and Windows 95/98, to write the Basic-language source file. (In Windows, look under Accessories.) At the DOS level, you can use the Edit program to write text files.

The compiler needs the basic program saved as a standard (MS-DOS) or ASCII test file because any special formatting and print codes that are unique to an individual word processor are not saved in the ASCII or DOS file types.

When you save the file, save it with a .bas suffix. For example, if you were saving a program named wink, you would save it as wink.bas. Saving the file with a .bas suffix is an option. The compiler will read the file with or without the .bas suffix. The .bas suffix will help you identify your PIC programs in a crowded directory.

Step 2: Using the compiler

The PICBasic compiler program is started by entering the command Pbc followed by the name of the text file. For example, if the text file we created is named wink.bas then at the DOS command prompt, we would enter

```
Pbc wink.bas
```

The Basic compiler compiles the text file into two additional files, a .asm (assembly language) file and a .hex (hexadecimal) file.

The wink.asm file is the assembly language equivalent of the Basic program. The wink.hex file is the machine code of the program written in hexadecimal numbers. It is the .hex file that is loaded into the PIC chip.

If the compiler encounters errors when compiling the Basic source code, it will issue a string of errors it has found and terminate. The errors listed need to be corrected in the Basic source code before the program will successfully compile.

Step 3: Programming the PIC chip

Connect the EPIC programmer to the computer's printer port using a DB25 cable. Start the DOS programming software. At a DOS command prompt, enter

```
EPIC
```

Figure 1.4 is a picture of the programming screen. Use the Open File option and select wink.hex from the files displayed in the dialog box. The file will load, and numbers will be displayed in the window on the left. Insert the 16F84 into the socket, then press the Program button. The PIC microcontroller is programmed and ready to go to work.

Ready, Steady, Go

This completes the overview. In Chap. 2 we will provide step-by-step instructions for writing the Basic text file and programming it into the PIC chip. You will find that the actual steps shown in Chap. 2 are not much more involved than the instructions in the overview. Purchase the components and let's go.

Parts List

PICBasic compiler	$ 99.95
EPIC programmer	$ 59.00
16F84 Microcontroller	$ 6.95
DB25 6-ft cable	$ 6.95
(1)4.0-MHz crystal	$2.50
(2) 22-pF capacitors	$0.10 each

Available from Images Company (see Suppliers Index).

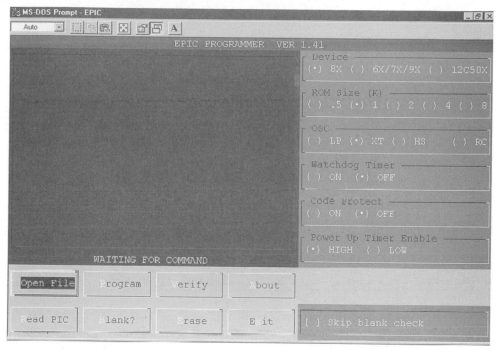

Figure 1.4 Screen shot of EPIC programming software (DOS). The program loaded is `wink.hex`.

(1) Solderless breadboard	RadioShack	PN#276-175
(1) 0.1-μF capacitor	RadioShack	PN#272-1069
(8) Red LEDs	RadioShack	PN#276-208
(8) 470-Ω resistors*	RadioShack	PN#270-1115
(1) 4.7-kΩ resistor	RadioShack	PN#271-1124
(8) 10-kΩ resistors	RadioShack	PN#271-1126
(1) 7805 voltage regulator	RadioShack	PN#276-1770
(2) Four-position PC-mounted switches	RadioShack	PN#275-1301
(1) 9-V battery clip	RadioShack	PN#270-325

Available at local RadioShack stores. Also available from James Electronics and JDR Micro Devices (see Suppliers Index).

---

*Also available in the 16-pin DIP package.

2

Software Installation
(Compiler and Programmer)

In this chapter, we provide step-by-step instructions for writing a text file for and programming a PIC microcontroller. We begin by loading the PICBasic compiler software onto your computer's hard drive and finish by programming and testing a PIC microcontroller chip.

Installing the PICBasic Compiler Software

The first thing we need to do is copy the PICBasic compiler software onto your computer's hard drive. If you are familiar with File Manager (Windows 3.X) or Windows Explorer, you can create subdirectories and copy all files with these tools. Step-by-step instructions are provided using DOS commands. You can, of course, use the same directory names outlined or make up your own.

The DOS instructions are provided to help the reader and to serve as a supplement to the installation directions provided with the software packages. The instructions are not meant as a DOS tutorial. More information on DOS commands can be found in any number of DOS manuals. Here is a list of DOS commands we will be using and what action they perform:

COMMAND	ACTION
cd	change directory
md	make directory
copy	copy files
xcopy	copy files and subdirectories
path	sets a search path for executable files
dir	directory

Before we can copy the files from our installation diskettes, we need a place to copy them to. For the PICBasic compiler we will create a subdirectory called pictools on the hard drive and copy the files on the diskette into it.

For Windows 3.X, use the File Manager program to create a subdirectory. For Windows 95/98, use the Windows Explorer program to create the subdirectory. Windows 95/98 users also have the option of opening a DOS window within the Windows environment. You can work inside the DOS windows using standard DOS commands.

You also have the option of restarting your computer in MS-DOS mode. In most cases you should be able to operate from the DOS window without problems.

Start the DOS window by selecting "MS-DOS Prompt" under the Programs menu under the Windows 95/98 "Start" button (see Fig 2.1). When the DOS window opens, you are probably starting the DOS session inside the Windows subdirectory. Your prompt may look like this: `C:/WINDOWS>`.

The DOS prompt provides vital information. The C: tells us we are on the C drive. The `/WINDOWS` tells us we are in the Windows subdirectory.

We want to work from the root directory of the computer's hard drive (usually the C drive). We accomplish this by using the `cd` (Change Directory) command.

The `cd..` command brings one up a single level in the directory hierarchy. Using the `cd\` brings one up to the root directory regardless of how deep (how many levels) one has moved into subdirectories. The root directory is the top of the directory hierarchy. From the Windows subdirectory either command

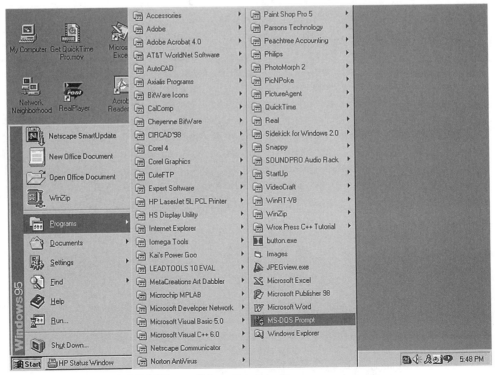

Figure 2.1   Selecting "MS-DOS Prompt" from Program menu.

may be used. Type `cd..` or `cd\` and hit the Enter key to back up a level in the directory.

```
C:/WINDOWS>cd..  or  C:/WINDOWS>cd\
```

(See Fig. 2.2.)

You should now be in the C drive root directory; the DOS prompt will change to `C:/>`. Once you are in the C drive's root directory, you can start the task at hand.

First, create a subdirectory on your hard drive called pictools. (If you don't like the name pictools, choose another name that is more to your liking.) At the DOS prompt, enter the "make directory" command (`md`) followed by a space and the name of the directory `pictools`. The complete command may look like this:

```
C:/> md pictools
```

This command creates a subdirectory called pictools. Now let's copy all the files on the PICBasic Compiler 3.5-in diskette into the new directory. Assuming that your 3.5-in disk drive is the A drive, at the DOS prompt, enter

```
C:/> xcopy a:*.* pictools /s
```

This command copies all the files on the diskette, including the subdirectories, into the pictools subdirectory (see Fig. 2.2). With the files safely

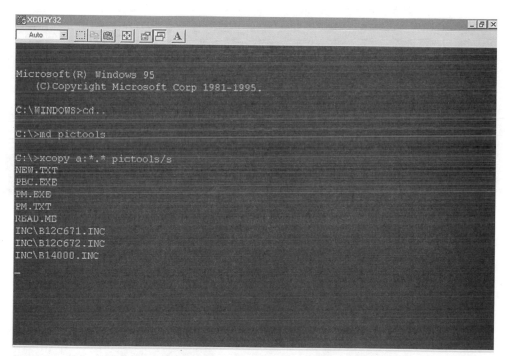

Figure 2.1 Using `cd` (change directory) and `md` (make directory) DOS commands at the DOS prompt.

loaded onto your hard drive, remove the diskette and store it in a safe place in case it is needed in the future.

Installing the EPIC Software

We are still in the root directory for the C drive. From here, create another subdirectory on your hard drive called epic. (If you don't like the name epic, choose another name that is more to your liking.) At the DOS prompt, enter

```
C:/> md epic
```

This creates another subdirectory called epic (Fig 2.3). Now let's copy all the files on the 3.5-in EPIC diskette into the new epic directory, as we have done for the compiler software. Again assuming that your 3.5-in disk drive is the A drive, at the DOS prompt, enter

```
C:/> xcopy a:*.* epic /s
```

This command copies all the files on the EPIC diskette, including the sub directories, into the epic subdirectory as shown in Fig. 2.3. With the files safely loaded onto your hard drive, remove the diskette and store it in a safe place in case it is needed in the future.

As you can see in the last figure, only two files were copied from the A drive into the epic directory. The reason is that the EPIC software is compressed in

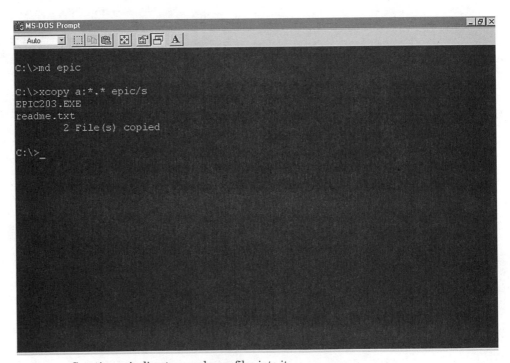

Figure 2.3 Creating epic directory and copy files into it.

the executable file epic203.exe. To run this program and decompress the files first move into the epic subdirectory by typing in

```
C:\ cd epic
```

at the DOS prompt and hitting the Enter key (see Fig. 2.4). The DOS prompt will change to C:\epic>. To run the program type in "epic203" at the DOS prompt, hit the Enter key (see Fig. 2.5). When I executed the program, it issued a warning (see the bottom of Fig. 2.5) that a readme.txt file already exists. Overwrite (y/n)? Answer y.

PIC Applications Directory

It would be a good idea if we created another subdirectory to store all our PICMicro application programs. This will keep all our pictools and epic directories clean, neat, and uncluttered. If you are performing these commands in the sequence they appear in the book you are currently in the epic subdirectory. We need to move back to the root directory before we do anything more. Use the cd (change directory) command to move back into the root directory, enter cd..

```
C:\epic> cd..
```

At the DOS prompt, hit the Enter key (see Fig. 2.6). The DOS will change to C:\> signaling we are in the root directory. We are ready to create another

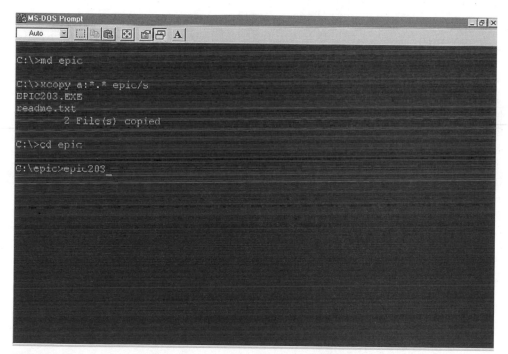

Figure 2.4 Running epic203.exe program to decompress the EPIC files.

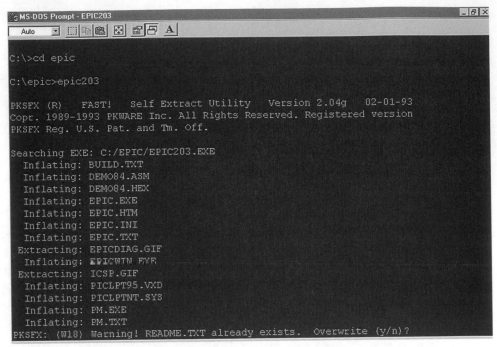

Figure 2.5   EPIC file list inflating. Answer to overwrite Readme.txt is yes (y).

subdirectory called applics. At the DOS prompt in the root directory type in md applics and hit the Enter key (see Fig. 2.7).

```
C:\>md applics
```

If you don't like the name applics choose another name more to your liking. We are almost ready to write our first program.

Path—The Final DOS Commands

Path is a DOS command that specifies a search path for program files. For example, the following command specifies that DOS is to search for files in the three directories listed in addition to the current directory:

```
path \;c:\pictools;c:\epic;c:\windows\command;
```

Each directory in the path command must be separated by a semicolon (;). The first backslash (\) indicates that the search should begin in the root directory of the current drive.

Using the above path command will allow you to run both the compiler (PBC) and the programmer (EPIC) from the applications directory (applics). This will streamline and simplify using both these programs. Without the path command you will have to copy files between directories and change directories to run programs.

Figure 2.6   Moving back to the root directory using the cd DOS command.

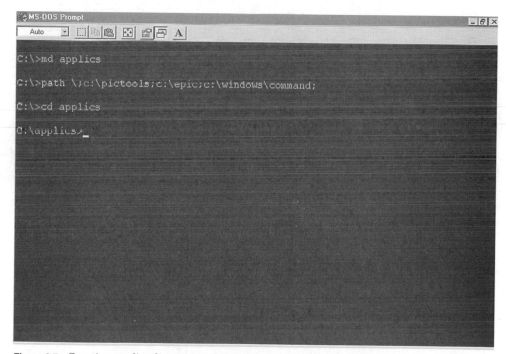

Figure 2.7   Creating applics directory and using the path DOS command.

The path command may be typed in at the DOS prompt and once you hit the Enter key will stay in effect for as long as the DOS window remains open (see Fig. 2.7).

```
C:\> path \;c:\pictools;c:\epic;c:\windows\command;
```

For those who are familiar with DOS commands, the path command can be made permanent by entering it into or adding onto an existing path command in the autoexec.bat file. For those who are not comfortable with DOS commands or changing the set-up of the computer, don't touch the autoexec.bat file. The autoexec.bat file is an important batch file that is run every time the computer starts or is reset.

If you want to learn more about DOS and the autoexec.bat file to make these changes, I recommend purchasing a tutorial book on DOS.

First Basic Program

We are now ready to write our first program. To write programs, you need a word processor or text editor. Windows users can use the Notepad program. DOS-level users can use the Edit program.

Since we want to store our programs in the subdirectory applics, the first step is to move into that directory. We will use the cd (change directory) command. Enter this at the DOS prompt (see Fig. 2.8).

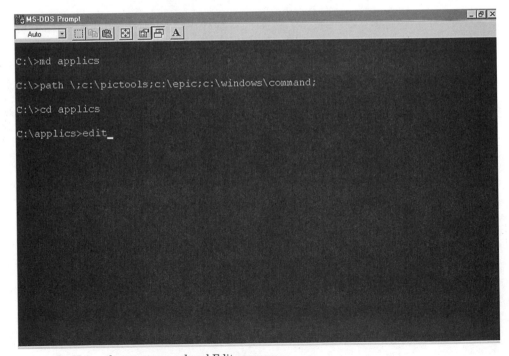

Figure 2.8 Using the cd command and Edit program.

```
C:\> cd applics
```

Once in this directory the prompt changes to

```
C:\applics>
```

In this example I will be using the free Edit program package with Windows to write the program. Start edit by typing edit at the command prompt (see Fig. 2.8).

```
C:\applics> edit
```

This starts the edit program (see Fig. 2.9). Enter this program in your word processor exactly as it is written:

```
'First Basic program to wink two LEDs connected to port B.
Loop: High 0      'Turn on LED connected to pin RB0
      Low 1       'Turn off LED connected to pin RB1
      Pause 500   'Delay for 0.5 s
      Low 0       'Turn off LED connected to pin RB0
      High 1      'Turn on LED connected to pin RB1
      Pause 500   'Delay for 0.5 s
      Goto loop   'Go back to loop and blink and wink LEDs forever
      End
```

See Fig. 2.10. Save the above as a text file in the applics directory. Use the Save function under the File menu. Name the file wink.bas (Fig. 2.11). The .bas suffix is optional. The compiler program will load and compile the file whether or

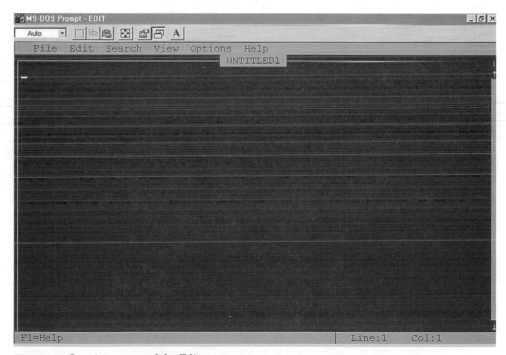

Figure 2.9 Opening screen of the Edit program.

not it has the .bas suffix. The suffix helps us remember what type of file it is. If, by accident, you saved the file as wink.txt don't get discouraged. You can do a Save As from the Edit program (under File menu) and rename the file wink.bas.

Remember, if you are using a different word processor, it is important to save the program as an ASCII or MS-DOS text file. The reason is that the compiler (the next step) requires the text file (the basic source code) in a DOS or ASCII file format. DOS and ASCII text files do not save any special formatting and print codes that are unique to individual word processors.

Compile

The PICBasic compiler must be run from DOS or from a DOS window within Windows. If you are still working in the same DOS session we started with, skip over the next two sentences. If you just started the DOS window, enter the path command as specified earlier. Use the cd commands to move into the applics directory.

We will run the PICBasic compiler from the applics directory, type the command pbc -p16f84 wink.bas at the DOS prompt, and hit the Enter key (see Fig. 2.12).

```
C:/APPLICS>pbc -p16F84 wink.bas
```

The compiler displays an initialization copyright message and begins processing the Basic source code (see Fig. 2.13). If the Basic source code is without

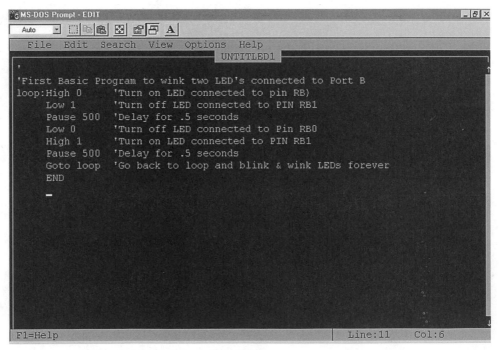

Figure 2.10 wink.bas program written using Edit.

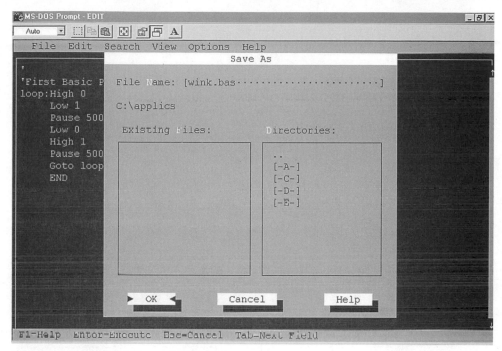

Figure 2.11 Saving text file as wink.bas.

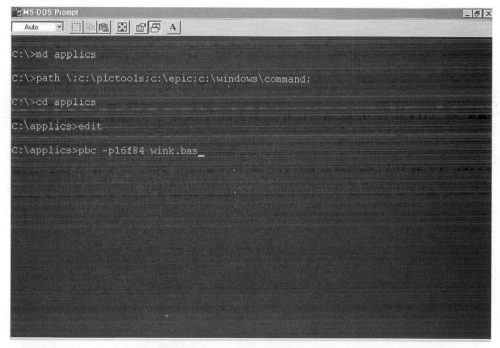

Figure 2.12 Running compiler on wink.bas file for the PIC 16F84.

errors (and why shouldn't it be?), the compiler will create two additional files. If the compiler finds any errors, a list of errors with their line numbers will be displayed. Use the line numbers in the error message to locate the line number(s) in the .bas text file where the error(s) occurred. The errors need to be corrected before the compiler can compile the source code correctly. The most common errors are with basic language syntax and usage.

You can look at the files by using the `dir` directory command. Type `dir` at the command prompt:

```
C:\APPLICS> dir
```

and hit Enter (see Fig. 2.14).

The `dir` command displays all the files and subdirectories within the subdirectory where it is issued. In Fig. 2.14 we can see the two additional files the compiler created. One file, the wink.asm file, is the assembler source code file that automatically initiates the macroassembler's compiling of the assembly code to machine-language hex code. The second file created is the hex code file, called wink.hex.

Programming the PIC Chip

To program the PIC chip, we must connect the EPIC programming carrier board (see Fig. 2.15) to the computer. The EPIC board connects to the printer port, also called the parallel port. (Either name may be used; they are both cor-

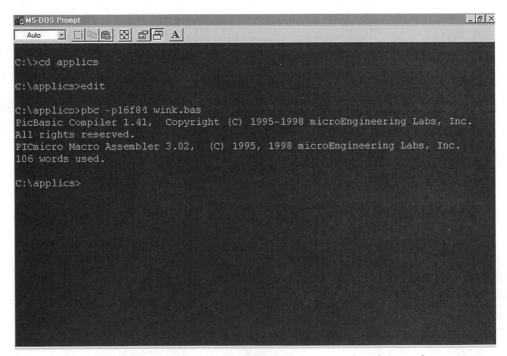

Figure 2.13 Compiler initialization messages and compiled program length in words.

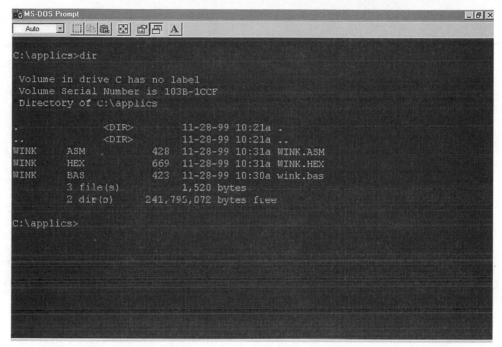

```
C:\applics>dir

 Volume in drive C has no label
 Volume Serial Number is 103B-1CCF
 Directory of C:\applics

 .               <DIR>        11-28-99 10:21a .
 ..              <DIR>        11-28-99 10:21a ..
WINK     ASM             428 11-28-99 10:31a WINK.ASM
WINK     HEX             669 11-28-99 10:31a WINK.HEX
WINK     BAS             423 11-28-99 10:30a wink.bas
         3 file(s)          1,520 bytes
         2 dir(s)     241,795,072 bytes free

C:\applics>
```

Figure 2.14 Looking at the two additional files (.hex and .asm) created using the DOS "dir" command.

rect.) A computer may contain up to four parallel (printer) ports. Each port is assigned a number from 1 through 4. The computer lists these ports as LPT1 to LPT4.

If your computer has only one printer port, disconnect the printer, if one is connected, and attach the EPIC programming board using a 6-ft DB25 cable.

When connecting the programming board to the computer, make sure there are no PIC microcontrollers installed on the board. If you have an ac adapter for the EPIC programmer, plug it in. If not, attach two fresh 9-V batteries. Connect the Batt ON jumper to apply power. The programming board must be connected to the printer port with power applied to the programming board before starting the software. Otherwise, the software will not register the programming board as connected to the printer port and will give the error message "EPIC Programmer Not Connected."

When power is applied and the programming board is connected to the printer port, the LED programming board on the EPIC programmer board may be on or off at this point. Do not insert a PIC microcontroller into the programming board socket until the EPIC programming software is running.

The EPIC programming board software

There are two versions of the EPIC software: EPIC.exe for DOS and EPICWIN.exe for Windows. The Windows software is 32-bit. It may be used

Figure 2.15 EPIC programming carrier board.

with Windows 95, Windows 98, and Windows NT, but not with Windows 3.X. It has been my experience that Windows 95 printer drivers often like to retain control of the printer (LPT1) port. If this is the case with your computer, the Windows epic program may not function properly, and you may be forced to use the DOS-level program. If you receive the error message "EPIC Programmer Not Connected" when you start the Windows EPIC program, you have the option of either troubleshooting the problem (see Troubleshooting EPIC Software, below) or using the EPIC DOS program.

Using the EPIC DOS version

If you are using Windows 95 or higher, you can open a DOS window or restart the computer in the DOS mode. If you are using Windows 3.XX, end the Windows session.

Troubleshooting EPIC Software: A Few Alternatives

If your computer has a single printer port (LPT1), you can add a second (LPT2) port for a nominal amount of money. An inexpensive printer card will cost about $20.00. If you have never added a card to your computer before, don't know the difference between an ISA or PCI, or never performed some type of system upgrade to your computer before, then I advise you to bring your computer to a computer repair/service store in your area and have them perform the upgrade.

There is no guarantee that the EPIC software will work with a second LPT port. You may still have to work at the DOS level to get it to function properly.

For instance, in order for me to run the EPIC DOS program from a DOS window in Windows 95 I needed to remove my HP (Hewlett-Packard) printer driver first (see Fig. 2.16). I opened the printer driver window and closed down (exited) the program.

Continuing with the wink.bas program

Assume we are still in the same DOS session and we have just run the PBC compiler on the wink.bas program. We are still in the applics directory. At the DOS prompt, type `epic` and hit enter to run the DOS version of the EPIC software (see Fig. 2.17).

If you are operating out of a DOS window you may get a device conflict message box as shown in Fig. 2.18. We want MS-DOS to control the LPT port so the EPIC programming software will work. Select the MS-DOS Prompt and hit the OK button.

EPIC's opening screen is shown in Fig. 2.19. Use the mouse to click on the Open button or press `Alt-O` on your keyboard. Select the wink.hex file (see Fig. 2.20). When the hex file loads, you will see a list of numbers in the window on the left (see Fig. 2.21). This is the machine code for your program. On the right-hand side of the screen are configuration switches that we need to check before we program the PIC chip.

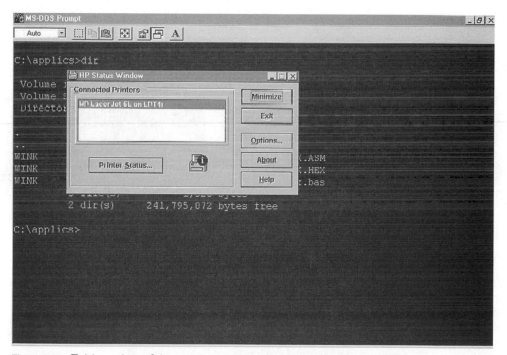

Figure 2.16   Exiting printer driver program.

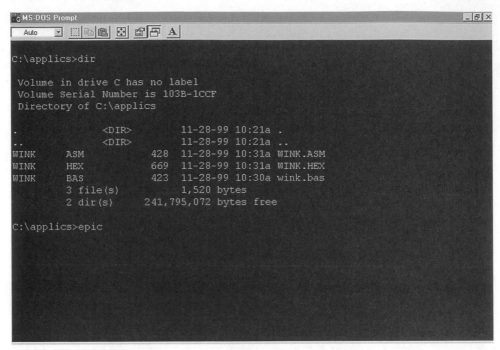

Figure 2.17 Running the EPIC program from MS-DOS Prompt window.

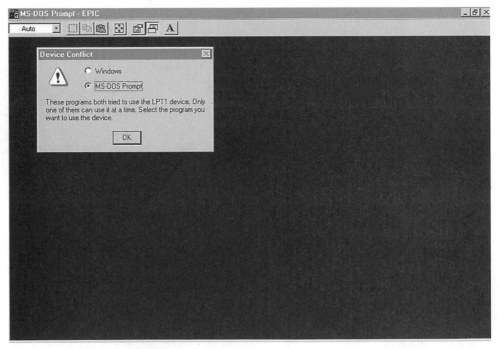

Figure 2.18 Device Conflict window.

Let's go through the configuration switches one by one.

Device: Sets the device type. Set it for 8X.

ROM Size (K): Sets the memory size. Choose 1.

OSC: Sets the oscillator type. Choose XT for crystal.

Watchdog Timer: Choose On.

Code Protect: Choose Off.

Power Up Timer Enable: Choose High.

After the configuration switches are set, insert the PIC 16F84 microcontroller into the socket. Click on Program or press Alt-P on the keyboard to begin programming. The EPIC program first looks at the microcontroller chip to see if it is blank. If the chip is blank, the EPIC program installs your program into the microcontroller. If the microcontroller is not blank, you are given the options of cancelling the operation or overwriting the existing program with the new program. If there is an existing program in the PIC chip's memory, write over it. The machine-language code lines are highlighted as the PIC is programmed. When the operation is finished, the microcontroller is programmed and ready to run. You can verify the program if you like by hitting (or highlighting) the Verify button. This initiates a comparison of the program held in memory with the program stored in the PIC microcontroller.

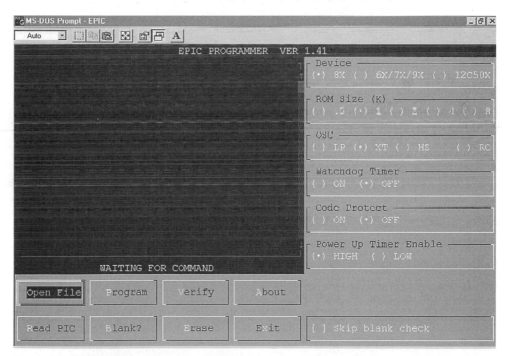

Figure 2.19   EPIC program's opening screen.

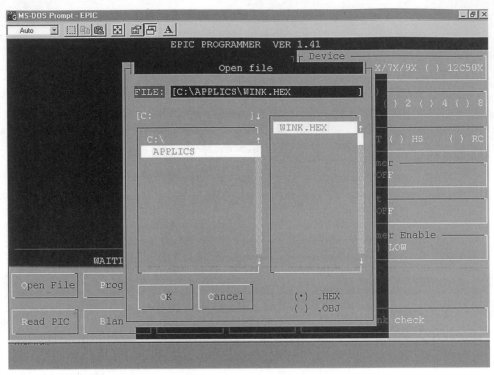

Figure 2.20   Selecting the wink.hex file.

Testing the PIC Microcontroller

If you purchased the components described in Chap. 1, you can quickly set up the test circuit. If not, you need to purchase those components now to continue.

The Solderless Breadboard

For those of us who have not dabbled in electronics very much, I want to describe the solderless breadboard (see Fig. 2.22). As the name implies, you can breadboard (assemble and connect) electronic components onto it without solder. The breadboard is reusable; you can change, modify, or remove circuit components on it at any time. This makes it easy to correct any wiring errors. The solderless breadboard is an important item for constructing and testing the circuits outlined in this book.

If you wish to make any circuit permanent, you can transfer the components onto a standard printed-circuit board and solder them together with the fore-knowledge that the circuit functions properly.

The internal structure of the board is shown in Fig. 2.23. The holes on the board are plugs. When a wire or pin is inserted into a hole, it makes intimate contact with the metal connector strip inside. The holes are properly spaced so that integrated circuits and many other components can be plugged right in.

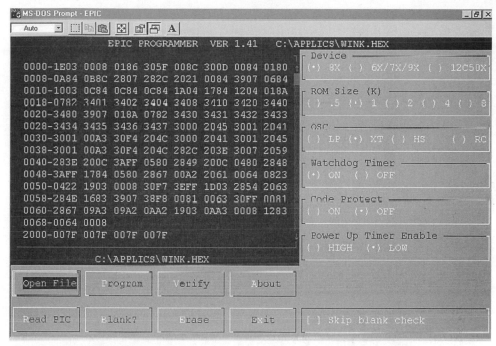

Figure 2.21   Wink.hex file loaded into EPIC program.

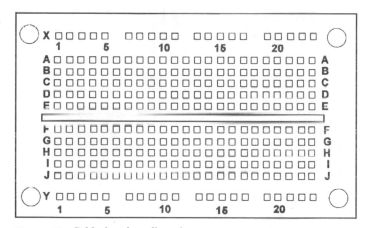

Figure 2.22   Solderless breadboard.

You connect components on the board using 22-gauge (solid or stranded) wire. I prefer to use stranded wire because it has greater flexibility.

The complete internal wiring structure of the board is shown in Fig. 2.24. The X and Y rows are typically used as power supply and ground connections. The columns below the X row and above the Y row are used for mounting components.

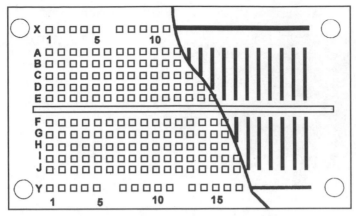

Figure 2.23   Internal structure of the solderless breadboard.

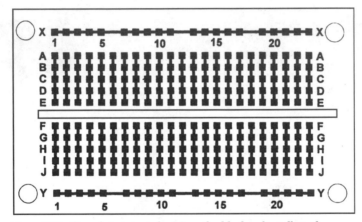

Figure 2.24   Complete internal wiring of solderless breadboard.

Three Schematics, One Circuit

Figures 2.25, 2.26, and 2.27 are identical schematics of our test circuit. I drew three schematics to help orient experimenters who may not be familiar with standard electrical drawings. Figure 2.25 shows how the PIC 16F84 microcontroller and components appear. There is a legend at the bottom that shows the electrical symbols and the typical appearance of the components. Figure 2.26 is a line drawing showing how the components appear mounted on the solderless breadboard. The labels in Fig. 2.26 point out each electrical component.

If you examine the placement of the components mounted on the solderless breadboard with its internal electrical wiring (Fig. 2.24), you can see how the components connect to one another and produce a circuit.

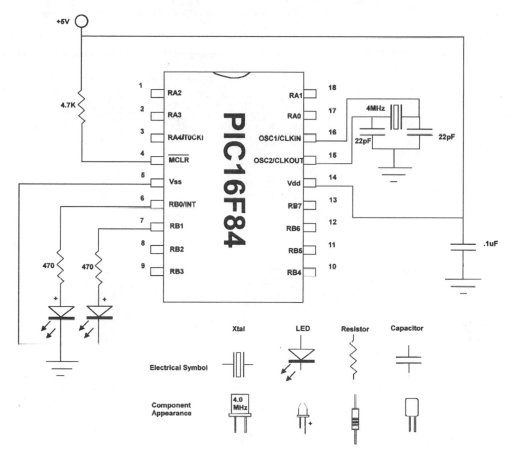

Figure 2.25 First view of components mounted on breadboard.

Figure 2.27 is the same schematic drawn as a standard electrical drawing, with the pin numbers grouped and oriented according to function. For the remainder of the book, standard electrical drawings will be used.

The schematic shows how few components are needed to get your microcontroller up and running. Primarily you need a pull-up resistor on pin 4 (MCLR), a 4-MHz crystal with two 22-pF capacitors, and a 5-V power supply.

The two LEDs and two current-limiting resistors connected in series with the LEDs are the output. They allow us to see that the microcontroller and program are functioning.

Assemble the components on the solderless breadboard as shown in the schematic (see Fig. 2.27). When you are finished your work should resemble Fig. 2.28.

While the specifications sheet on the 16F84 states that the microcontroller will operate on voltages from 2 to 6 V, I provide a regulated 5-V power supply for the circuit. The regulated power supply consists of a 7805 voltage regulator and two filter capacitors.

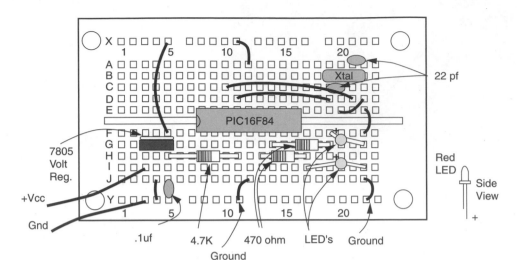

Figuro 2.26 Second view of components mounted on breadboard.

* Capacitors connected to crystals are 22pF

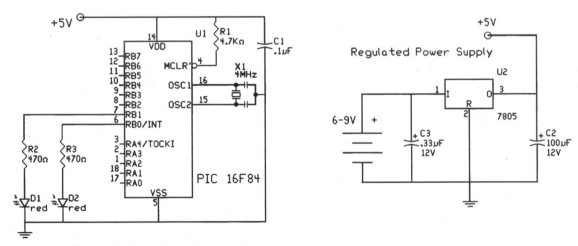

Figure 2.27 Electrical schematic of wink project.

Wink

Apply power to the circuit. The LEDs connected to the chip will alternately turn on and off. Wink... wink... Now you know how easy it is to program these microcontrollers and get them up and running.

As you gain experience, using the compiler and programmer will become second nature. You won't even consider them as steps anymore. The real challenge will be writing the best PICBasic programs possible. And that is as it should be.

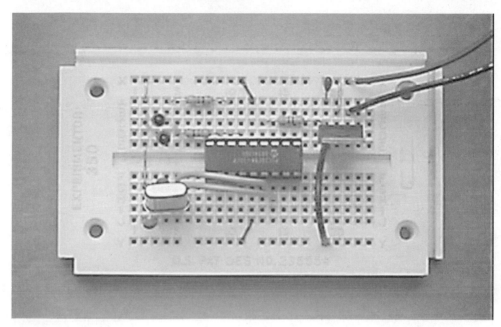

Figure 2.28   Photograph of wink project.

Troubleshooting the Circuit

There is not too much that can go wrong here. If the LEDs don't light up, the first thing I would check is the orientation of the LEDs. If they are put in backward, they will not light.

Next check your ground wires. See the jumper wires on the right-hand side of the solderless breadboard. They bring the ground up to the two 22-pF capacitors.

Check all your connections. Look back at Figs. 2.23 and 2.24 to see how the underlying conductive strips relate to the push-in terminals on top of the board.

Chapter Review

Before we move on to the next chapter, let's review the important steps we have learned in programming a PIC microcontroller. We will not review the installation, because that's typically a one-time job.

This review assumes we are working from DOS.

Step 1. Upon entering DOS, if you are not in the root directory, move to the root directory using the cd command cd.. or cd\>

Step 2. At the DOS prompt enter the path command:

```
C:\> path \;c:\pictools;c:\epic;c:\windows\command;
```

Step 3. Enter the applics directory using the cd command:

```
C:\ cd applics
```

Step 4. Start your word processor or the Edit program:

```
C:\applics> edit
```

Step 5. Write the Basic program. Save the program as an ASCII-type text file. Save the file with a .bas suffix (e.g., wink.bas). Note that .bas is optional.

Step 6. From the applics directory, run the PICBasic compiler. The command line for compiling the wink.bas program for a PIC16F84 microcontroller is as follows:

```
C:\applics> pbc -p16F84 wink.bas
```

The -p16F84 tells the compiler to compile the program for this particular microcontroller. The compiler is capable of writing for a large number of PIC microcontrollers you will find listed in the compiler manual. The .bas after the program name is optional.

The compiler reads the .bas file and, if it finds no errors, generates two files, wink.asm and wink.hex. If the compiler finds an error, the program needs to be corrected and recompiled.

Step 7. Connect the EPIC programming board to the computer's parallel (printer) port. Turn on the EPIC board power supply.

Step 8. From the applics subdirectory run the EPIC DOS program.

```
C:\applics> epic
```

Load the program's .hex file. Insert a PIC 16F84 into the programming socket on the programming board. Highlight the Program button and hit the Enter key on your keyboard to program the PIC microcontroller.

Remove the PIC microcontroller chip and test it.

In the next chapter, we will look at output-programmable attributes of the 16F84.

Parts List

Same components as listed for Chap. 1.

3

PIC 16F84 Microcontroller

In this chapter, we begin looking at the PIC16F84 microcontroller in greater detail. What we learn about this microcontroller is applicable to most of the other PIC microcontrollers. So, while it appears that we are focusing only on the PIC16F84 microcontroller, just keep in mind that it is representative of all the other PIC microcontrollers.

What advantages do other PIC microcontrollers have over the PIC 16F84? Primarily, they boil down to two different advantages: cost and options. For instance, the 16C61, while similar to the 16F84, is half the cost of the 16F84. However, the 16C61 is an OTP (one-time programmable) microcontroller. That's not the type of chip you want to work with when designing and proto-typing programs and circuits because chances are that you will need to trouble-shoot and reprogram the chip before everything is perfected and functions the way you want it to function.

After the prototyping stage is completed, the 16C61 may be the preferable choice for the mass production of a product. Let's suppose you create a commercial product that uses a PIC microcontroller and you are going to mass-produce it. Switching from the 16F84 to the 16C84 will save you quite a bit of money.

Aside from cost, other PIC microcontrollers have unique features that the PIC16F84 doesn't have, such as analog-to-digital converters, more RAM, or more I/O lines. In this book we will focus on the 16F84, but in my next book we shall look at these other microcontrollers.

Harvard Architecture and Memory-Mapped I/O

PIC microcontrollers use Harvard architecture. That simply means that the memory on the PIC microcontrollers is divided into program memory and data memory. The devices also use separate buses to communicate with each memory type. The Harvard architecture has an improved bandwidth in comparison to traditional computers that use the von Neumann architecture. (von

Neumann architecture accesses data and memory over the same bus.) The Harvard architecture allows for other enhancements. For instance, instructions may be sized differently than 8-bit-wide data.

The data memory in the PIC microcontroller can be further broken down into general-purpose RAM and the special function registers (SFRs).

The registers on the PIC 16F84 are mapped in the data memory section at specific addresses. The PICBasic language allows us to read and write to these registers as if they were standard memory bytes. This is an important concept to learn and remember. We read and write to the registers (memory location) using the Basic language's Peek (read) and Poke (write) commands. By writing numbers into the chip's registers, we program the chip I/O (via the registers) and have it perform the functions we need.

Although we read and write to the registers using our familiar decimal numbers, to understand what happens inside the register with those numbers requires a fundamental understanding of the binary number system.

Binary Fundamentals

To access the PIC chip registers efficiently, a little binary goes a long way. Binary isn't difficult to learn because there are only two values. That's what the word *binary* means: "based on two," as in the two numbers 0 and 1. Binary 0 and 1 can also be compared to an electrical signal controlled by a switch that has two values, off (0) and on (1). In binary, a digit is called a *bit*, which stands for *bi*nary dig*it*.

An 8-bit digital number, or *byte*, can hold any decimal value between 0 and 255. In hexadecimal notation, these same values (0 to 255) are expressed as 00 to FF. We are not going to be learning hex (the hexadecimal number system), primarily because we don't need to use hexadecimal notation to write Basic programs. It's nice to know hexadecimal notation in the grand scheme of things because it is used at times, but it is not essential. What is essential at this point is to gain an understanding of binary; stay focused on this. When you understand the binary number system completely, then (and only then) if you are still interested in hexadecimal notation, there is a quick tutorial in the Appendix.

The CPU in the PIC 16F84 uses an 8-bit data bus (pathway). The registers in the PIC chip are also 8 bits wide. Thus, a byte is the perfect size to access the PIC chip registers. We will read from and write to the PIC microcontroller's registers using the decimal numbers between 0 and 255, which can be contained in one 8-bit byte.

However, when we write a decimal number into a register, the microcontroller can only see the binary equivalent of that decimal number (byte). To understand what's happening inside the register, we need to be able to look at the binary equivalent of the decimal number (byte) also. Once we can do this, our ability to effectively and elegantly program the PIC microcontroller is greatly enhanced.

Examine Table 3.1. This table shows the decimal- and binary-number equivalents for the numbers 0 through 31. Using this information, the binary numbers from 32 to 255 can be extrapolated.

In the table, each decimal number on the left side of the equal sign has its binary equivalent on the right side. So when we see a decimal number, the microcontroller will see the same number as a series of 8 bits (8 bits to a byte).

Registers and Ports

The PIC 16F84 contains two I/O ports, port A and port B. Each port has two registers associated with it, the TRIS (Tri State) register and the port register address itself.

The TRIS register controls whether a particular pin on a port is configured as an input line or an output line. Once the ports are configured the user may then read or write information to the port using the port register address. (The terms *pins* and *lines* off the PIC 16F84 mean the same thing and are used interchangeably throughout the text.)

On port B we have eight I/O lines available. On port A only five I/O lines are available to the user. Figure 3.1 shows the relationship between a binary number and the two PIC microcontroller registers that control port B. Let's look at the binary-number side. Notice that for each move of the binary 1 to the left, the exponential power of 2 is increased by 1.

TABLE 3.1   Binary Number Table

0 = 00000000	16 – 00010000	32 = 00100000
1 = 00000001	17 = 00010001	.
2 = 00000010	18 = 00010010	.
3 = 00000011	19 = 00010011	.
4 = 00000100	20 = 00010100	64 = 01000000
5 = 00000101	21 = 00010101	.
6 = 00000110	22 = 00010110	.
7 = 00000111	23 = 00010111	.
8 = 00001000	24 = 00011000	128 = 10000000
9 = 00001001	25 = 00011001	.
10 = 00001010	26 = 00011010	.
11 = 00001011	27 = 00011011	.
12 = 00001100	28 = 00011100	255 = 11111111
13 – 00001101	29 = 00011101	
14 = 00001110	30 = 00011110	
15 = 00001111	31 = 00011111	

Port B

TRISB　Decimal 134　86 Hex　Port B　Decimal 6　06 Hex

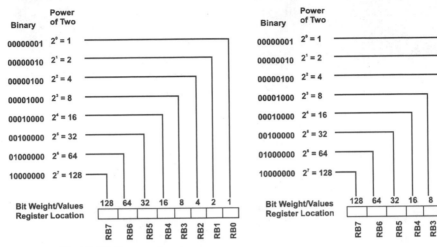

Figure 3.1　Port B I/O lines and registers.

Bit #	Decimal	Binary
Bit 0	1 =	00000001
Bit 1	2 =	00000010
Bit 2	4 =	00000100
Bit 3	8 =	00001000
Bit 4	16 =	00010000
Bit 5	32 =	00100000
Bit 6	64 =	01000000
Bit 7	128 =	10000000

These are relevant numbers, because each position identifies a bit location and bit weight within the 8-bit byte.

For instance, suppose we wanted to write binary 1s at the RB7 and RB4 locations. To do so, we add their bit weights together, in this case 128 (RB7) and 16 (RB4), which equals 144. The binary equivalent of decimal number 144 is 10010000. If you slide that number into the register, you will see that the binary 1s are in the RB7 and RB4 positions. Remember this; it is important.

The open TRISB register shown in Fig. 3.1 may be used to examine numbers placed in the TRISB. The port B register may be used to examine numbers placed at the port B register.

Notice the correlation between the register bit locations, bit weights, and port B I/O pins. This correspondence between the bit number, bit weight, and the I/O line is used to program and control the port. A few examples will demonstrate this relationship.

Using the TRIS and port registers

The TRIS register is a 1-byte (8-bit) programmable register on the PIC 16F84 that controls whether a particular I/O pin is configured as an input or an output pin. There is a TRIS register for each port. TRISA controls the I/O status for the pins on port A and TRISB controls I/O status for the pins on port B.

If you place a binary 0 at a bit location in TRISB for port B, the corresponding pin location on port B will become an output pin. If you place a binary 1 at a bit location in the TRISB, the corresponding pin on port B will become an input pin. The TRISB data memory address for port B is 134 (or 86h in hex).

After port B has been configured using TRISB register, the user can read or write to the port using the port B address (decimal number 6).

Here is an example. Suppose we want to make all port B lines output lines. To do so we need to put a binary 0 in each bit position in the TRISB register. So the number we would write into the register is decimal 0. Now all our I/O lines are configured as output lines.

If we connect an LED (light-emitting diode) to each output line, we can see a visual indication of any number we write to the port B. If we want to turn on the LEDs connected to RB2 and RB5, we need to place a binary 1 at each bit position on the port B register. To accomplish this we look at the bit weights associated with each line. RB2 has a bit weight of 4, and RB5 has a bit weight of 32. We add these numbers together (4 + 32 = 36) and write that number into the port B register.

When we write the number 36 into the port B register, the LEDs connected to RB2 and RB5 will light.

To configure port A, we use the TRISA register, decimal address 133 (see Fig. 3.2). On port A, however, only the first 5 bits of the TRISA and the corresponding I/O lines (RA0 to RA4) are available for use. Examine the I/O pin out on the 16F84 and you will find that there are only five I/O pins (RA0 to RA4) corresponding to port A. These pins are configured using the TRISA register and used through the port A address.

Register	Memory location (hexadecimal)	Memory location (decimal)
Port A	05h	5
Port B	06h	6
TRISA	85h	133
TRISB	86h	134

Port A

TRISA Decimal 133 85 Hex   Port A Decimal 5 05 Hex

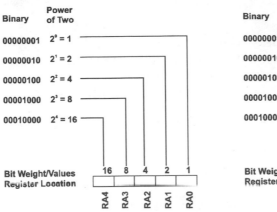
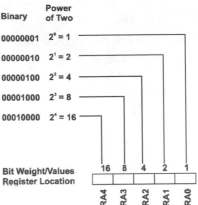

Figure 3.2 Port A I/O lines and registers.

On power-up and reset, all the I/O pins of port B and port A are initialized (configured) as input pins. Of course, we can change this with our program.

Here is another example. Let's configure port B so that bit 7 (RB7) is an input pin and all other pins are output lines. To place binary 0s and 1s in the proper bit location, we use the bit weights shown in Fig. 3.1. For instance, to turn bit 7 on (1) and all other bits off (0), we would write the decimal number 128 into the TRISB for port B. In Basic, the command to write to a register is the Poke command. The program line to write the decimal value 128 into the TRISB register will look like

```
Poke 134,128
```

The number after the Poke command is the memory address that the command will write to—in this case, 134, which is the data memory address of the TRISB for port B. The next number, after a comma is the value we want to write in that memory address. In this case, it is 128.

Look at the binary equivalent of the decimal number 128:

$$1\ 0\ 0\ 0\ 0\ 0\ 0\ 0$$

Mentally place each 1 and 0 into the TRISB register locations shown in Fig. 3.1. See how the 1 fits into the bit 7 place, making that corresponding line an input line, while all other bit locations have a 0 written in them, making them output lines.

So by pokeing (writing) this location with a decimal number that represents a binary number containing the proper sequence of bits (0s and 1s), we can configure the pins in the port to be any combination of outputs and inputs that we might require. In addition, we can change the configuration of the port "on the fly" as the program is running.

To summarize, pokeing a binary 1 into the TRIS register turns that corresponding bit/pin on the port to an input pin. Likewise, pokeing a binary 0 will turn the bit into an output.

Accessing the Ports for Output

Once the port lines have been configured (input or output) using the TRIS register, we can start using the port. To output a binary number at the port, simply write the number to the port using the Poke command. The binary equivalent of the decimal number will be outputted as shown in our first example. To output a high signal on RB2, we could use this command:

```
Poke 6, 4
```

where 6 is the memory address for port B and 4 is the decimal equivalent of the binary number we want to output. Reading input information on the ports will be discussed in Chap. 4.

Electrical Binary, TTL, and CMOS

When a pin on port B (RB0 to RB7) is configured as an input line, the microcontroller can read (via the Peek command) the electrical voltage present on that input pin to determine its binary value (0 or 1).

When a pin on a port is configured as an output, the microcontroller can raise the voltage on that pin to +5 V by placing a binary 1 at the bit location on the port. A binary 0 at the bit location will output a zero voltage.

When a pin (or bit) is set to 1 it may be called "on," "set," or "high." When a bit is set to 0 that may be called "off," "cleared," or "low."

In TTL logic, electrically, a binary 1 is equal to a positive voltage level between 2 and 5 V. A binary 0 is equal to a voltage of 0 to 0.8 V. Voltages between 0.8 and 2 V are undefined.

CMOS has a slightly different definition. Input voltages within 1.5 V of ground are considered binary 0, whereas input voltages within 1.5 V of the +5-V supply are considered binary 1.

Digital logic chips (TTL and CMOS) are available in a number of subfamilies—CMOS: 4000B, 74C, 74HC, 74HCT, 74AC, 74ACT; and TTL: 74LS, 74ALS, 74AS, 74F. These differences become important when you need to make different logic families talk to one another.

CMOS devices swing their outputs rail-to-rail so +5-V CMOS can drive TTL, NMOS, and other +5-V-powered CMOS directly. [The exception to this is old-fashioned CMOS (4000B/74C).] TTL devices on the other hand may not output sufficient voltage for a CMOS device to see a binary 1, or "high" signal.

This could have been a problem, since the PIC 16F84 is a CMOS device. The designers of the PIC were thoughtful enough to buffer the I/O lines with TTL buffers, thus allowing the PIC I/O lines to accept TTL input levels while outputting full CMOS voltages. This allows us to directly connect TTL logic devices, as well as CMOS devices, to our PIC microcontroller without difficulty.

Counting Program

To illustrate many of these concepts, I have written a simple Basic program. It is a binary counting program that will light eight LEDs connected to port B's eight output lines.

The counting program will light the LEDs in the sequence shown in the binary number table. Each binary 1 in a number in the table will be represented with a lit LED. Every 250 ms ($\frac{1}{4}$ s), the count increments. After reaching the binary number 255 (the maximum value of a byte), the sequence repeats, starting from zero.

Counting in binary by one

Enter the following program into your word processor exactly as it is written. Save it as an ASCII text file (or DOS text) with the .bas extension.

```
'Program 3.1, Binary Counting
'Initialize variables
Symbol TRISB = 134      'Assign TRISB for port B to decimal value of 134
Symbol PortB = 6        'Assign the variable portB to the decimal value 6
'Initialize Port(s)
Poke TRISB, 0           ' Set port B pins to output
loop:
For B0 = 0 to 255
Poke PortB, B0          'Place B0 value at port to light LEDs
Pause 250               'Without pause, counting proceeds too fast to see
Next B0                 'Next B0 value
Goto loop
'end
```

Let's look at the program and decipher it line by line. The first two lines are comments, which begin with a single quotation mark (').

```
'Program 3.1, Binary Counting
'Initialize variables
```

The compiler ignores all text following a quotation mark. You should use comments liberally throughout your Basic code to explain to yourself what you are doing and how you are doing it. What appears obvious to you when you are writing a program will become obscure a few months later. All comments are stripped when the program is compiled into .hex and .asm files, so you can add as many comments as you like—they do not take up any program space.

The following two lines initialize two important variables. The TRISB is assigned the decimal value of 134 and the port B represents the port B address, decimal value of 6, for subsequent use in the program. Technically, we don't need to initialize these variables. We could write the decimal equivalent (number 134) instead of using the TRISB variable when needed by the program. So if we wanted, we could write POKE 134, XX instead of POKE TRISA, XX. However, when initializing variables, especially in more complex programs, using a mnemonic variable for decimal values makes writing the programs and following the logic easier and less error-prone.

```
Symbol TRISB = 134     'Assign TRISB for port B to decimal value of 134
Symbol PortB = 6       'Assign the variable PortB the decimal value 6
```

The variable TRISB now represents a decimal value of 134, and the variable PortB now represents a decimal value of 6. Hereafter in the program, we can refer to TRISB without needing to remember its numerical value, and the same is true for PortB. The comments following each instruction provide valuable information on what each command is doing.

```
'Initialize Port(s)
```

This is a comment that tells what is to follow.

```
Poke TRISB, 0          ' Set all port B pins to output
```

The following line is the command that initializes port B with a zero, making all the port B lines output lines.

```
loop:
```

This line contains a label called loop. The word *loop* is clearly identifiable as a label because of the colon (:) following the word. Labels can be referred to in the program for jumps (Goto's and on value) and subroutines (Gosub's).

```
For B0 = 0 to 255
```

This line defines our variable B0. In standard Basic, this line would probably read for x = 0 to 255. In this line we are using one of PICBasic's predefined variables, B0. The 16F84 has a limited amount of RAM that can be accessed for temporary storage. In the case of the 16F84, there are 68 bytes of RAM. Of this total area of 68 bytes of RAM, 51 bytes are available for user variables and storage.

User-available RAM

RAM may be accessed as bytes (8-bit numbers) or words (16-bit numbers). PICBasic has predefined a number of variables for us. Byte-sized variables are named B0, B1, B2, B3,..., B51. Word-sized variables are named W0, W1, W2,..., W25. The byte and word variables use the same memory space and overlap one another.

Word variables are made up of two byte-sized variables. For instance, W0 uses the same memory space of variable bytes B0 and B1. Word variable W1 is made up of bytes B2 and B3, and so on.

Word variables	Byte variables	Bit
W0	B0	Bit0, Bit1,..., Bit 7
	B1	Bit8, Bit9,..., Bit15
W1	B2	
	B3	
W2	B4	
	B5	
...	...	
W39	B78	
	B79	

The variables may be used for number storage. The variables may also be given a name that has meaning in the program by using the command Symbol. For instance we could rename our variable B0 to X to make this program read more like a standard Basic-language program.

We used the Symbol command in the beginning of the program to store the variables TRISB and PortB.

If you write a program that uses more variables than the PIC microcontroller has RAM to store, the PICBasic compiler will not generate an error when it compiles the program. Your program will simply not function properly. It is up to you to keep track of how many variables are being used in the program. For the 16F84, you may use up to 51 bytes or 25 words, or a combination of both.

When you program other PIC microcontrollers, check their data sheets to see how much RAM they have available.

```
Poke PortB, B0          'Place B0 value at port to light LEDs
```

This line writes the value B0 to PortB. Any binary 1s in the number are displayed by a lit LED.

```
Pause 250               'Without pause, counting proceeds too fast to see
```

This line makes the microcontroller pause for 250 ms ($1/4$ s), allowing us enough time to see the progression.

```
Next B0                 'Next B0 value
```

This line increments the value of B0 and jumps up to the For B0 = 0 to 255 line. If the value of B0 equals the end value declared in the line (255), the program drops to the next line.

```
Goto loop
```

When B0 equals 255, the for-next loop is finished and this line directs the program to jump to the label *loop*, where the B0 value is reinitialized and the number counting repeats, starting from zero.

Figure 3.3 shows the schematic for this program. Figure 3.4 is a photograph of this project. Notice that I used a second solderless breadboard to hold the resistors and LEDs so I wouldn't have to squeeze everything onto a single breadboard.

Programming challenge

Rewrite the last program, renaming the B0 variable X. This will make the program appear more like a "standard" Basic-language program. The programming answer is given in the Appendix.

Counting Binary Progression

The last program was informative. It showed us how to output electrical signals via port B. Those electrical signals may be used for communication and/or control. As we shall learn in future chapters, an electrical signal off one pin can control just about any household electrical appliance.

We are not yet finished with our simple circuit. With a little programming modification, we can have the same circuit perform a binary progression instead of binary counting. What's the difference between a binary progression and counting? The binary progression lights each single LED in sequence, starting with the first LED, then the second LED, and so on until the last LED is lit, after which the progression repeats. When the LEDs are arranged in a straight line, it looks as if the lit LED travels from one end of the straight line to the other. If the LED lights were arranged in a circle, the lit LED would appear to travel in a circle.

```
'Program 3.2, Binary Progression Counting
'Initialize variables
Symbol TRISB = 134      'Assign TRISB port B to 134
Symbol PortB =   6      'Assign the variable PortB the decimal value 6
'Initialize Port(s)
Poke TRISB, 0           ' Set port B pins to output
loop:
B0 - 1                  ' Set variable to 1 to start counting
```

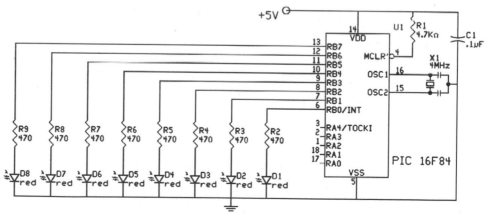

Figure 3.3 Schematic for LED counting project.

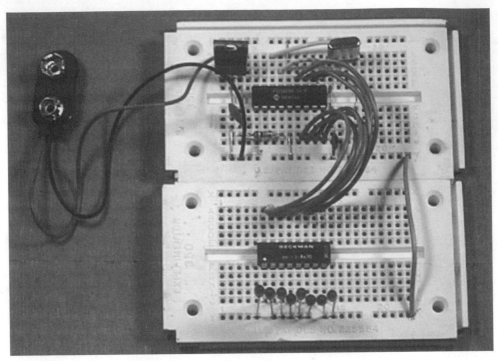

Figure 3.4 Photograph of LED counting project.

```
B1 = 0                    ' Set variable to 0
Poke PortB, B0            'Place B0 value at port to light LEDs
Pause 250                 'Without pause, this proceeds too fast to see
For B2 = 0 to 6
B1 = B0 * 2               'Calculate next binary progressive number
B0 = B1                   'Set B0 to new value
Poke PortB, B0            'Place new value at port to light LEDs
Pause 250                 'Without pause, counting proceeds too fast to see
Next B2                   'Next loop value
Goto loop
```

Programming challenge

Can you rewrite the binary sequence program above so that the LEDs light in
sequence, but do not turn off until all the LEDs are lit, after which the cycle
repeats? The answer is given in the Appendix.

Basic High and Low Commands

The way we have defined outputting information thus far is the most powerful and elegant way to do so. However, it is not the easiest. The PICBasic compiler has two Basic-language commands for outputting information on any of
the Port B pins, High and Low.

These commands are limited to port B; they will not work on port A lines. So if your knowledge of the Basic language did not include the Poke command and an understanding of binary, you would be unable to use the five I/O lines to port A.

The High command makes the specified pin output high. The pin so defined is automatically made into an output pin. This works only with port B pins 0 to 7. The command structure is as follows:

```
High Pin
```

So the command

```
High 0
```

makes pin 0 an output pin and sets it high (+5 V).

The Low command makes the specified pin output low. The pin so defined is automatically made into an output pin. This works only with port B pins 0 to 7. The command structure is as follows:

```
Low Pin
```

So the command

```
Low 0
```

makes Pin 0 an output pin and sets it low (0 V).

The High and Low commands are quick and easy commands to use and do have their usefulness. Real programming power and versatility is obtained using the Poke command. Don't believe it? Try rewriting our simple binary counting programs using just the High and Low commands. Call me when you're done.

As a sample program that uses the High and Low commands, here is the first program we worked with from Chap. 2.

```
Loop: High 0      ' Turn on LED connected to pin RB0
      Low 1       ' Turn off LED connected to pin RB1
      Pause 500   ' Delay for 0.5 s
      Low 0       ' Turn off LED connected to pin RB0
      High 1      ' Turn on LED connected to pin RB1
      Pause 500   ' Delay for 0.5 s
      Goto loop   ' Go back to loop and blink and wink LEDs forever
      End
```

Programming Review

Before we proceed to the next chapter, let's take time to review the key programming concepts we have used in the last few programs.

Comments

Use comments liberally when writing your programs. Use them to describe the logic and what the program is doing at that particular point. This will allow you to follow and understand the program's logic long after you have written (and probably forgotten) the program. Comments begin with a single quotation mark (') or with the word REM. The compiler ignores all characters on the line following the quotation mark or the keyword REM.

Identifiers

Identifiers are names used for line labels and symbols. An identifier may be any sequence of letters, digits, and underscores, but it must not start with a digit.

Identifiers may be any number of characters in length; however, the compiler will recognize only the first 32 characters.

Identifiers are not case-sensitive, so the labels LOOP:, Loop:, lOOP:, and loop: will be read equivalently.

Line labels

Labels are anchor points or reference points in your program. When you need the program to jump to a specific program location through either a Goto, Gosub, or Branch, use a label. Labels are easy to use. Use a descriptive word (identifier) for a label, such as the word *loop:* that we used in Programs 3.1 and 3.2. *Loop* is descriptive inasmuch as it shows the main loop point for the program.

Labels are identifiers followed by a colon (:).

Symbols

Symbols help to make our programs more readable. They use identifiers to represent constants, variables, or other quantities. Symbols cannot be used for line labels.

In our programs, we used the symbol TRISB to represent the decimal number 134. The number 134 is the data memory address for the TRISB register for port B. The symbol PortB represents the memory address for port B. Symbols are easier to remember than numbers. Here are a few examples of the symbol keyword usage.

```
Symbol      Five = 5          'Symbolic constant
Symbol      Number = W2       'Named word variable
Symbol      Bvalue = BIT0     'Named bit variable
Symbol      AKA = Bvalue      'An alias for Bvalue
```

Variables

Variables are temporary storage for your program. A number of variables have been predefined for usage in your programs. Byte-sized (8-bit) variables are named B0, B1, B2, and so on. Word-sized (16-bit) variables are named W0, W1, W2, and so on.

Remember these variables overlap and use the same memory space.

The word variables are made up of two byte-sized variables. For instance, the 16-bit W0 is made up of the two smaller 8-bit B0 and B1 variables, W1 is made up of B2 and B3, and so on.

Any of these variables can be renamed to something more appropriate to a program using the Symbol command.

Take special note of variables B0 and B1 because we can read their individual bits (Bit0, Bit1,..., Bit15). The ability to read the bits in these variables is very attractive for many bit-checking applications. Since the word variable W0 is composed of the two bytes B0 and B1, the bit-checking commands will also work with this word variable.

Read the specification sheets on the PIC microcontrollers to determine how much free RAM is available. The 16F84 has 68 bytes of free RAM, of which 51 bytes are available to the user.

Reading Input Signals

The programs we have written thus far have dealt only with outputting binary signals that we can see using the LEDs. While this is extremely important, it is also just as important to be able to read input off the lines. The status (binary state 0 or 1) of a line (signal) may be a digital signal or a switch. In the next chapter, we will examine inputting signals to our PIC microcontroller.

4

Reading I/O Lines

In the last chapter, we studied outputting binary numbers (information) to port B and viewing the information using miniature red LEDs. In this chapter, we will be inputting binary information.

The ability of our microcontroller to read the electrical status of its pin(s) allows the microcontroller to see the outside world. The line (pin) status may represent a switch, a sensor, or electrical information from another circuit or computer.

The Button Command

The PICBasic compiler comes equipped with a simple command to read the electrical status of a pin called the Button command. The Button command, while useful, has a few limitations. One limitation of this command is that it may be used only with the eight pins that make up port B. The I/O pins available on port A cannot be read with the Button command. Another limitation is that you cannot read multiple pin inputs at once, but only one pin at a time.

We will overcome these Button command limitations later on, using the Peek command. But for the time being, let's use and understand the Button command.

As the name implies, the button command is made to read the status of an electrical "button" switch connected to a port B pin. Figure 4.1 shows two basic switch schematics, *a* and *b*, of a simple switch connected to an I/O pin.

The Button command structure is as follows:

```
Button Pin, Down, Delay, Rate, Var, Action, Label
```

Pin	Pin number (0 to 7), port B pins only.
Down	State of pin when button is pressed (0 or 1).
Delay	Cycle count before auto-repeat starts (0 to 255). If 0, no debounce or auto-repeat is performed. If 255, debounce but no auto-repeat is performed.
Rate	Auto-repeat rate (cycles between auto-repeats), (0 to 255).

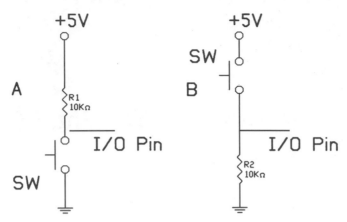

Figure 4.1 Switches connected to I/O line (pin).

Var	Byte sized variable used for delay/repeat countdown. Should be initialized to 0 prior to use.
Action	State of button in order to perform Goto (0 if not pressed, 1 if pressed).
Label	Point at which execution resumes if *Action* is true.

Let's take another look at the switch schematic in Fig. 4.1 before we start using the button switch to visualize how the switches affect the I/O pin electrically.

The switch labeled A in Fig. 4.1 connects the I/O pin to a 15-V power supply through a 10,000-Ω resistor. With the switch open, the electrical status of the I/O pin is kept high (binary 1). When the switch is closed, the I/O pin connects to ground, and the status of the I/O pin is brought low (binary 0).

The switch labeled B in Fig. 4.1 has an electrical function opposite the switch labeled A. In this case, when the switch is open, the I/O pin is connected to ground, keeping the I/O pin low (binary 0). When the switch is closed, the I/O pin is brought high (binary 1).

In place of a switch, we can substitute an electrical signal, high or low, that can also be read using the Button command.

Typically the Button command is used inside a program loop, where the program is looking for a change of state (switch closure). When the state of the I/O pin (line) matches the state defined in the *Down* parameter, the program execution jumps out of the loop to the Label portion of the program.

Debouncing a switch

Debouncing is a term used to describe eliminating noise from electric switches. If you took a high-speed electrical photograph, off an oscilloscope, of an electric switch closing or opening, the switch's electric contacts make and break electric connections many times over a brief (5- to 20-ms) period of time. This making and breaking of electric contacts is called *bounce* because the contacts can be easily visualized as bouncing together and separating. Computers, microcontrollers, and many electronic circuits are fast enough to see this bouncing as multiple switch closures (or openings) and respond accordingly. These responses are typically called *bounce errors*. To circumvent these bounce errors, debounce circuits and techniques have been developed.

The Button command has debounce features built in.

Auto-repeat

If you press a key on your computer keyboard, the character is immediately displayed on the monitor. If you continue to hold the key down, there is a short delay, following which a stream of characters appears on the screen. The Button command's auto-repeat function can be set up the same way.

Button example

To read the status of a switch off I/O pin 7, here is the command we will use in the next program:

```
Button 7, 0,254,0,B1,1,loop
```

The next program is similar to Program 3.1 in Chap. 3, inasmuch as it performs binary counting. However, since we are using PB7 (pin 7) as an input and not an output, we lose its bit weight in the number we can output to port B. The bit weight for pin 7 is 128, so without pin 7 we can display only numbers up to decimal number 127 (255 − 128 = 127). This is reflected in the first loop (pin7/bit 7 − 128).

The program contains two loops; the first loop counts to 127, and the current number's binary equivalent is reflected by the lit LEDs connected to port B. The loop continues to count as long as switch SW1 remains open.

When SW1 is closed, the Button command jumps out of loop 1 into loop 2. Loop 2 is a noncounting loop in which the program remains until SW1 is reopened. You can switch back and forth between counting and noncounting states.

Figure 4.2 is a schematic of our button test circuit. The difference between this schematic and the schematic used in Chap. 3 is that we added a 10-kΩ resistor and switch to pin 7 and removed the LED (see Fig. 4.3).

```
'Program 4.1
Symbol TRISB = 134          'Set TRISB to 134
Symbol PortB = 6            'Set PortB to 6
'Initialize Port(s)
Poke TRISB,128              'Set port B pins 1-6 to output, pin 7 to input
loop1:                      ' Counting loop
For B0 = 0 to 127
Poke PortB, B0              'Place B0 value at port B to light LEDs
B1 = 0                      'Set Button variable to 0:
Pause 250                   'Without pause, counting is too fast to see
Button 7,0,254,0,B1,1,loop2 ' Check Button status—if closed, jump
Next B0                     'Next B0 value
Goto loop1
loop2:                      'Second loop—not counting
```

* Capacitors connected to crystals are 22pF.

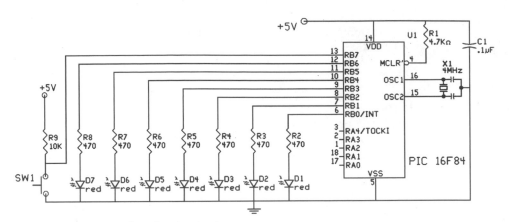

Figure 4.2 Schematic of test button circuit.

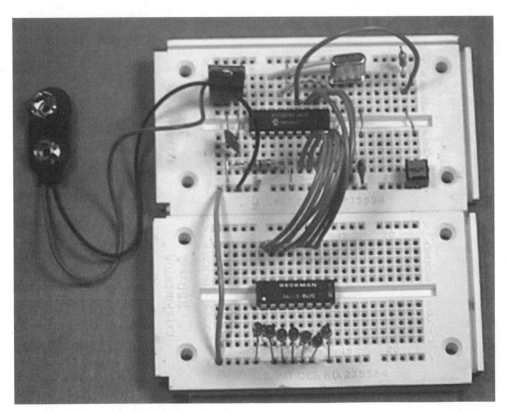

Figure 4.3 Photograph of test button circuit.

```
Poke portB,0                       'Turn off all LEDs
B1= 0                              'Set Button variable to zero before use
Button 7,1,254,0,B1,1,loop1       'Check Button status—if open, jump back
Goto loop2
```

When the program is run, it begins counting. When the switch is closed, all the LEDs turn off and it stops counting. When the switch is opened, the counting resumes, starting from 0.

Dynamic Changes

The previous program used one switch to start and stop the counting function. Now let's use two switches to dynamically modify the program as it is running. What dynamic modification could we make? How about changing the timing delay?

Now we need two switches: one switch to decrease the delay to make counting go faster, and the other switch to increase the delay to make it go slower. To connect another switch, we need to borrow another port B line. I decided to use line PB6, to monitor another switch status (see schematic in Fig. 4.4 and photograph of project in Fig. 4.5). The switch connected to PB7 incrementally increases the timing delay to a 1-s maximum time. The switch connected to PB6 incrementally decreases the delay to approximately 10 ms. At a 10-ms time delay, the LEDs will be counting so fast it will appear as if all the LEDs were lit simultaneously.

```
'Program 4.2
Symbol TRISB = 134                 'Set TRISB to 134
Symbol TRISB = 6                   'Set PortB to 6
B1 - 0:B2 = 0
Symbol delay = W4                  'Initialize delay variable
W4 = 250                           'Initialize variable to 250-ms delay
'Initialize Port(s)
Poke TRISB,192                     'Set port B pins 0-5 to output, pins 6 and 7 to
                                   'input
loop1:                             'Main counting loop
For B0 = 0 to 63
Poke PortB, B0                     'Place B0 value at port to light LEDs
Pause delay                        'Without pause, counting is too fast to see
B1 = 0: B2 = 0                     'Set to 0 before using in Button command
Button 7,0,1,0,B1,1,loop2         'Check SW1 status - if closed jump
                                   'delay the same
Button 6,0,1,0,B2,1,loop3         'Check SW2 status—if closed, jump
                                   'delay the same
Next B0                            'Next B0 value
Goto loop1
loop2:                             'loop2 increases time delay
delay = delay + 10                 'Increase delay by 10 ms
B1 = 0: Pause 100
Button 7,1,1,0,B1,1,loop1         'Check button status—if opened, jump
                                   'increasing
If delay > 1000 Then hold1         'don't go over 1-s delay
Goto loop2
```

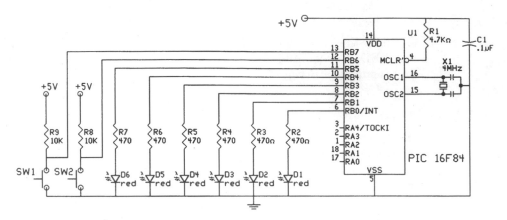

Figure 4.4   Schematic of multiple button test circuit.

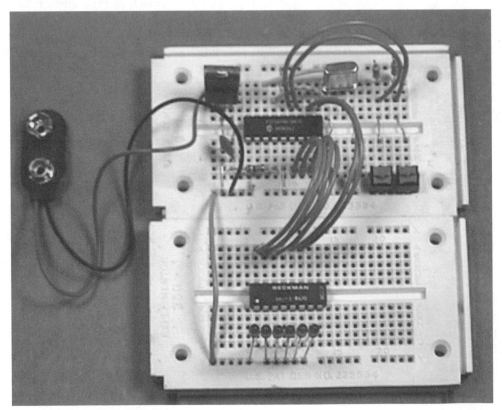

Figure 4.5   Photograph of multiple button test circuit.

```
loop3:                        'Second loop decreases delay
delay = delay - 10            'Decrease delay by 10 ms
B2 = 0:Pause 100
Button 6,1,1,0,B2,1,loop1     'Check button status—if opened, jump
                              'decreasing
If delay < 20 Then hold2      'Not less than 10-ms delay
Goto loop3
hold1:                        'Maintain delay at upper limit
delay = 1000                  'Maximum delay
Goto loop2                    'Return to the calling loop
hold2:                        'Maintain delay at lower limit
delay = 10                    'Minimum delay
Goto loop3                    'Return to the calling loop
```

Program 4.2 Features

We have introduced a few new program features; let's review them now before we continue. Primarily we wrote a standard Basic-language decision-making (If-Then) command line.

If..Then

In this program, the If..Then is used to limit the upper and lower limits of the timing delay between increments in the binary counting. In standard Basic, this line would appear as

```
If delay > 1000 Then delay = 1000
```

This line would effectively limit the upper limit to 1000 ms or 1 s. However, in the PICBasic compiler language, the If..Then command cannot be used in this way. While we still have the ability to test two variables with a comparison, the Then portion of the If..Then is essentially a Goto.

```
If comparison (and/or comparison) Then Label
```

If the condition is true, the program will perform a Goto to the label mentioned after Then. If the condition is false, the program continues on the next line after the If..Then. Let's look at this using a few examples. Suppose the variable delay is equal to 1010. The line

```
If delay > 1000 then hold1
```

would cause the program execution to jump to the label hold1 and continue on from there.

On the other hand, if the delay variable is equal to 990, no action would be taken by the line

```
If delay > 1000 then hold1
```

and program execution would continue on to the next line.

Unlike the standard Basic language, another statement may not be placed after Then. You can only use a *Label* after Then.

For instance the line

```
if delay > 1000 then delay = 1000
```

is not allowed in PICBasic.

Like the standard Basic language, there are multiple comparisons available. You can use the following comparisons in the If..Then command line:

Var (<, <=, =, <>, >=, >) *Value*

Comparison	Meaning
<	Less than
<=	Less than or equal to
=	Equal to
<>	Not equal to
>=	Greater than or equal to
>	Greater than

All comparisons must be unsigned. The compiler supports only unsigned types. The variable in the comparison must appear on the left.

In this program, we limit the delay value in the If..Then line by jumping to a small subroutine called `hold1` if that condition is true. The `hold1` subroutine performs the limit function for us.

```
If delay > 1000 Then hold1
...
hold1:
delay = 1000          'Maximum delay
Goto loop2      'Return to the calling loop
```

This is a somewhat convoluted way to accomplish the task needed, but it works.

Word variable

Notice that our delay variable is a 2-byte word variable W4. Can you figure out the reason why we need a 2-byte variable? If you think it's because a 1-byte variable can hold only a maximum number of 255, and our delay can go up to 1000, you are right. In order to hold a number greater than 255, we need to use at least 2 bytes. So what is the maximum number our 2-byte variable can hold? The answer is 65,535. If we used the maximum delay our 2-byte W4 variable allowed, we would have to wait more than a minute (65.5 s) for each increment in the count.

The Variables Used in Button

The Button command line states that the byte variable used for delay/repeat countdown should be set to initialized to zero prior to use.

Multiple Statements—Single Line

As with the standard Basic language, we can place multiple statements on a single line. The statements must be separated by a colon (:). The fourth line in program 4.2 is an example: B1 = 0:B2 = 0. Here we set the values of variables B1 and B2 to zero.

Peek

We can also use the Peek command to check the status of any input line. The advantages of the Peek command are as follows: Using Peek, one can read the five I/O lines of port A (or the eight I/O lines of port B) at once. This increases the versatility of the PIC chip and allows our program to be more concise (less convoluted), shorter, and easier to read.

To emphasize these points, let's rewrite our last program using the Peek command. This program uses the schematic shown in Fig. 4.6.

Looking at the schematic we can see the RA0 and RA1 lines are normally kept high (15 V), binary 1 through the 10-kΩ resistor. When a switch is closed, it connects the pin to ground and the line is brought down to (ground) binary 0.

A photograph of this project is shown in Fig. 4.7.

```
'Program 4.3
Symbol TRISB = 134          'Set Data Direction Register port B
Symbol TRISA = 133          'Set Data Directory Register port A
Symbol PortB = 6            'Initialize PortB to 6
Symbol PortA = 5            'Initialize PortA to 5
Symbol delay = W3           'Set up delay variable
W3 = 250                    'Initialize delay value
'Initialize Port(s)
Poke TRISB,0                'Set port B pins as output
```

* Capacitors connected to crystals are 22pF.

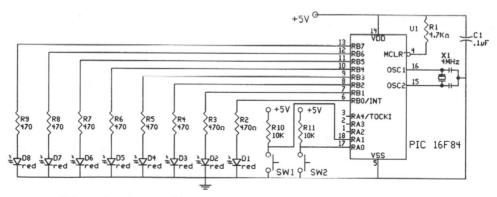

Figure 4.6 Schematic using Port A lines for push buttons.

Figure 4.7 Photograph of project using Port A lines for buttons.

```
Poke TRISA,3              'Set pin 1 and pin 2 of port A as input
loop1:                    'Counting loop
For B2 = 0 to 255
Poke PortB, B2            'Place B2 value at port to light LEDs
pause 250                 'Without pause, counting proceeds too fast to
                          'see
Peek PortA,B0             'Peek SW status on PortA
If bit0 = 0 Then loop2    'If SW1 is closed, jump to loop2
If bit1 = 0 Then loop3    'If SW2 is closed, jump to loop3
Next B2                   'Next B2 value
Goto loop1                'Repeat
loop2:                    'Increment binary counting delay
Poke PortB,0              'Turn off all LEDs
delay = delay + 10        'Increase delay by 10 ms
pause 100                 'Delay or timing changes too quickly
If delay > 1000 Then hold1 'Not over 1-s delay
Peek PortA,B0             'Peek SW1 status on PortA
If bit0 = 1 Then loop1    'If opened, jump back to loop1
Goto loop2                'Repeat
loop3:                    'Decrement binary counting delay
Poke PortB,0             'Turn off all LEDs
Peek PortA,B0            'Peek SW2 status on PortA
If bit 1 = 1 Then loop1   'If opened, jump back to loop1
```

```
delay = delay - 10          'Decrease delay by 10 ms
If delay < 10 Then hold2    'If less than 10 ms, hold at 10
Goto loop3                  'Repeat
hold1:                      'Hold at 1-s routine
delay = 990
Goto loop2
hold2:                      'Hold at 10-ms routine
delay - 20
Goto loop3
```

Program 4.3 may appear as large as Program 4.2, but there is a major difference: Program 4.3 is utilizing both ports on the PIC 16F84. We can easily see the impact this has by looking at the schematic in Fig. 4.6.

In this schematic, we are using the entire port B to light eight LEDs. Since we can use the entire port B, we can count to decimal 255. We can do this because we can connect the two switches to port A. Incidentally, I could have reduced the size of this program by eliminating the lines for the TRISA setup.

If you remember, upon start-up or reset, all port lines are configured as input lines. Since this is how we need port A set up, I could have eliminated those lines dealing with the TRISA. Instead I decided to show a standard port A setup, even though it wasn't needed in this particular application, as an example setup.

New Features

Program 4.3 introduced a few new features. The first new command used is the Peek command. The Peek command structure is as follows: the command Peek is followed by a memory address, then a comma, then a storage variable.

```
Peek Address, Var
```

As its name implies, the Peek command allows one to view (or peek at) the contents of a specified memory address. Typically the memory address "peeked at" is one of the PIC microcontroller's registers. The peeked value is stored in a variable *Var* defined in the command.

In this program we peeked at the input lines on port A. (Remember, the lines on port A cannot be read using the Button command.) The Peek command allows us to look at the two input lines on port A simultaneously.

```
Peek PortA, B0
```

The Peek command can read an entire byte (8 bits) at once; or, as in the case of port A 5 bits, only the lower 5 bits of the peeked value are relevant.

Bit0 .. Bit15

The first 2 bytes of RAM memory, B0 and B1, are special. This is because we can test the bit values contained in each byte. If you remember, for byte B0, the bit variables are predefined as Bit0 through Bit7. For byte B1, the predefined bit variables are Bit8 to Bit15.

The next two commands used in the program use the bit variables to allow us to look at and test the individual bits that make up byte B0.

```
If bit0 = 0 Then loop2
If bit1 = 0 Then loop3
```

The logic of the program follows, just before we tested the bit values we peeked PortA and saved the results in variable B0.

```
Peek PortA, B0
```

Then we tested the bits in variable B0 using the predefined Bit0 and Bit1 variables in the If..Then commands to see if a switch was closed on either line. If it was, the program jumped to the proper subroutine.

Programming challenge

Rewrite Program 4.1 using the Peek command instead of the Button command. The solution is in the Appendix.

Basic Input and Output Commands

In our programs, we directly wrote (using the Poke command) to the PIC microcontroller TRIS registers (A or B) to set various pins to be either input or output lines. By Pokeing the TRIS register, we are able to configure the eight pins to port B at one time. In addition, and more important, we can configure the five open pins on port A as well.

However, the PICBasic compiler has two Basic commands for making pins either input or output lines. These commands are Input and Output. Unfortunately, these two commands work only on port B pins.

```
Input Pin
```

This command makes the specified pin an input line. Only the pin number itself, i.e., 0 to 7, is specified (e.g., *not* Pin0).

Sample usage:

```
Input 2        'Makes pin 2 an input line.
```

The opposite of the input command is the output command,

```
Output Pin
```

This command makes the specified pin an output line. Only the pin number itself, i.e., 0 to 7, is specified (e.g., *not* Pin0).

Sample usage:

```
Output 0       'Makes pin 0 an output line.
```

Okay, we have established a foundation on PIC microcontrollers that allows us to work on applications. But before we do, I want to offer a few tips that will make programming easier.

ZIF Adapter Sockets

If you have been programming the sample programs into a 16F84, you probably realize by now that it is troublesome and inconvenient to insert the 16F84 microcontroller into and remove it from the standard socket on the EPIC programming board.

There is an 18-pin ZIF (zero-force insertion) socket adapter for the EPIC board that allows you to remove and insert the 16F84 easily and quickly (see Fig. 4.8).

I recommend purchasing the ZIF adapter because it saves a considerable amount of time and hassle, not to mention bent pins.

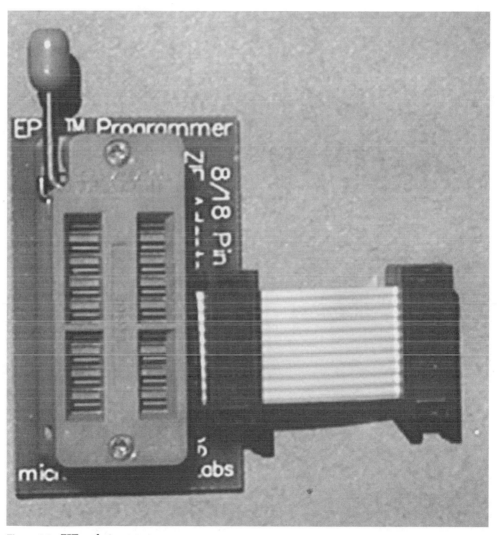

Figure 4.8   ZIF sockets.

ZIF Socket

While this is not as critical as the ZIF socket adapter for the EPIC programming board, I also placed an 18-pin ZIF socket on my solderless breadboard. This allowed me to move the PIC between testing and programming boards quickly.

AC Adapter

The stock EPIC programming board requires two fresh 9-V batteries. An ac adapter that eliminates batteries is available. These three additions to your programming arsenal will make programming PIC microcontrollers easier.

Parts List

Same components as Chaps. 1 and 3.

Additional components

(2) 10KΩ $\frac{1}{4}$-W resistors

(2) PC mount push-button switches, normally open (N.O.)

Optional components

ZIF socket adapter for programming board

ZIF socket for solderless breadboard

AC adapter for programming board

PICBasic Language Reference

Before we proceed further into PICMicro applications and projects, this chapter is devoted to the PICBasic language commands that are available to us. The following is a list of PICBasic commands with a quick description. This is followed by a complete description of each command, in alphabetical order.

Branch	Computed Goto (equivalent to On...Goto)
Button	Input on specified pin.
Call	Call assembly language subroutine at specified label.
Eeprom	Define initial contents of on-chip EEPROM.
End	Stop program execution and enter low-power mode.
For..Next	Execute a defined For–Next loop.
Gosub	Call Basic subroutine at specified label.
Goto	Jump program execution to specified label.
High	Make specified pin an output and bring it high.
I2cin	Read bytes from I^3C device.
I2cout	Write bytes to I^2C device.
If..Then	Compare and Goto if specific condition is true.
Input	Make specified pin an input.
Let	Perform math and assign result to variable.
Lookdown	Search table for value.
Lookup	Fetch value from table.
Low	Make specified pin an output and bring it low.
Nap	Power-down processor for short period of time.
Output	Make specified pin an output.
Pause	Delay (1-ms resolution).
Peek	Read byte from PIC microcontroller register.
Poke	Write byte to PIC microcontroller register.
Pot	Read potentiometer on specified pin.

Pulsin   Measure pulse width (10-μs resolution).

Pulsout   Generate pulse (10-μs resolution).

Pwm   Output pulse-width-modulated signal from pin.

Random   Generate pseudorandom number.

Read   Read byte from on-chip EEPROM.

Return   Return from subroutine.

Reverse   Reverse I/O status of pin; input becomes output and vice versa.

Serin   Asynchronous serial input (8N1).

Serout   Asynchronous serial output (8N1).

Sleep   Power-down processor (1-s resolution).

Sound   Generate tone or white noise on specific pin.

Toggle   Make specified pin an output and toggle state.

Write   Write byte to on-chip EEPROM.

Branch

```
Branch Offset, (Label0, Label1,...,LabelX)
```

Uses *Offset* (byte variable) to index into the list of labels. Execution continues at the indexed label according to the *Offset* value. For example, if *Offset* is 0, program execution continues at the first label specified (*Label0*) in the list. If the *Offset* value is 1, then execution continues at the second label in the list.

```
Branch B8, (label1, label2, label3)
```

If B8 = 0, then program execution jumps to label1.

If B8 = 1, then program execution jumps to label2.

If B8 = 2, then program execution jumps to label3.

Button

```
Button Pin, Down, Delay, Rate, Var, Action, Label
```

Pin   Pin number (0 to 7), port B pins only.

Down   State of pin when button is pressed (0 or 1).

Delay   Delay before auto-repeat begins, 0 to 255.

Rate   Auto-repeat rate, 0 to 255

Var   Byte-sized variable needed for delay repeat. Should be initialized to 0 before use.

Action   State of pin to perform Goto (0 if not pressed, 1 if pressed).

Label   Point at which program execution continues if *Action* is true.

Figure 5.1 shows the schematic for two styles of switches that may be used with this command.

```
Button 0,0,255,0,B0,0,Loop
```

This checks for a button pressed on pin 0 and does a Goto to Loop if it is not pressed.

Call

```
Call Label
```

Jump to an assembly language routine named *Label*.

```
Call storage
```

This jumps to an assembly language subroutine named storage. Before program execution jumps to the storage routine, the next instruction address after the Call instruction is saved. When the Return instruction is given by the storage routine, the previously saved instruction address is pulled, and program execution resumes at the next instruction after Call.

Eeprom

```
Eeprom    Location, (constant, constant,..., constant)
```

This command stores constants in consecutive bytes in on-chip EEPROM. It works only with PIC microcontrollers that have EEPROM, such as the 16F84 and 16C84.

```
Eeprom 4, (10, 7, 3)
```

This stores 10, 7, and 3, starting at EEPROM location 4.

End

```
End
```

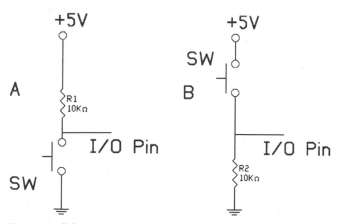

Figure 5.1 Schematic switches used for Button command.

This command terminates program execution and enters low-power mode by executing continuous Nap commands.

For..Next

```
For Index = Start to Stop (Step (-) Inc)
      Body
Next Index
```

Index is the variable holding the initial value *Start*.

Start is the initial value of the variable. *Step* is the value of the increment. If no *Step* value is specified, it is incremented by 1 each time a corresponding Next statement is encountered. The *Step* increment value may be positive or negative. If *Step* and *Inc* are eliminated, the step defaults to positive 1.

Stop is the final value. When *Index* = *Stop*, the corresponding Next statement stops looping back to For, and execution continues with the next PICBasic statement.

Body is Basic statements that are executed each time through the loop. *Body* is optional and may be eliminated, as is the case in time-delay loops.

```
For B0 = 0 to 127
Poke PortB, B0           'Place B0 value at port to light LEDs
Next B0                  'Next B0 value
```

This program snippet is from Chap. 4.

Gosub

```
Gosub Label
```

Program execution jumps to statements beginning at *Label*. A Return statement must be used at the end of the *Label* subroutine to return program execution to the statement following the Gosub statement.

Gosub statements may be nested. However, nesting should be restricted to no more than four levels.

```
Gosub wink               'Execute subroutine named wink
  .                      'Program execution returns to here
  .                      'Other programming goes here
  .
wink:                    'Label wink
High 0                   'Bringing pin 0 high lights LED
Pause 500                'Wait 1/2 s
Low 0                    'Bringing pin 0 low turns off LED
Return                   'Return to main routine
```

Gosub nesting

Nesting is the term used to describe a second Gosub routine called from within a previous Gosub routine. Because of memory limitations Gosubs can only be nested to a maximum of four levels deep.

Goto

```
Goto Label
```

Program execution jumps to statements beginning at *Label*.

```
        Goto loop        'Program execution jump to statements beginning at
                         'loop.
loop:
For b0 = 1 to 10
Poke portB, b0
Next
```

High

```
High Pin
```

This command makes the specified pin an output pin and brings it high (+5 V). Only the pin number itself, 0 to 7, is specified in the command. This command works only on port B pins.

```
High 2           'Make pin 2 (RB2) an output pin and bring it high
                 '  (+5 V)
```

I2cin

```
I2cin Control, Address, Var (, Var)
```

This command allows one to read information from serial EEPROMs using a standard two-wire I^{2}C interface. The second (, *Var*) shown in the command is used only for 16-bit information. Information stored in a serial EEPROM is nonvolatile, meaning that when the power is turned off, the information is maintained.

Here is a list of compatible serial EEPROMs.

Device	Capacity	Control	Address size
24LC01B	128 bytes	01010xxx	8 bits
24LC02B	256 bytes	01010xxx	8 bits
24LC04B	512 bytes	01010xxb	8 bits
24LC08B	1K bytes	01010xbb	8 bits
24LC16B	2K bytes	01010bbb	8 bits
24LC32B	4K bytes	11010ddd	16 bits
24LC65	8K bytes	11010ddd	16 bits

bbb = block selects bits (each block − 256 bytes).
ddd = device selects bits.
xxx = don't care.

The high-order bit of the *Control* byte is a flag that indicates whether the address being sent is 8 or 16 bits. If the flag is low (0), then the address is

8 bits long. Notice that EEPROMs 24LC01B to 24LC16B have the flag set to zero (0).

The lower 7 bits of *Control* contain a 4-bit control code, followed by the chip select or address information. The 4-bit control code for a serial EEPROM is 1010. Notice that in all the listed serial EEPROMs, this same 4-bit control code follows the high-bit flag.

The I²C data and clock lines are predefined in the main PICBasic library. The I²C lines are pin 0 (data) and pin 1 (clock) of port A. The I²C lines can be reassigned to other pins by changing the equates at the beginning of the I²C routines in the PBL.INC file.

Figure 5.2 is a schematic of a 24LC01B connected to a PIC 16F84.

```
Symbol control = %01010000
Symbol address = B6                    'Set variable address to B6
       address = 32                    'Set address to equal 32
       I2cin control, address, B2      'Read data from EEPROM
                                       'address 32 into B2
```

I2cout

```
I2cout Control, Address, Value (, Value)
```

The I2cout command allows one to write information to serial EEPROMs using a standard two-wire I²C interface. The second (, *Value*) shown in the command is used only for 16-bit information. Information stored in a serial EEPROM is nonvolatile, meaning that when the power is turned off, the information is maintained.

When writing to a serial EEPROM, one must wait 10 ms (device-dependent) for the Write command to complete before communicating with the device becomes possible. If one attempts a I2cin or I2cout before the Write (10 ms) is complete, the access will be ignored. Using a Pause 10 statement between multiple writes to the serial EEPROM will solve this problem.

Control and *Address* are used in the same way as described for the I2cin command.

```
Symbol control = %01010000
Symbol address = B6                       'Set variable address to B6
       address = 32                       'Set address to equal 32
       I2cout control, address, (16)      'Write data number 16 to the 'EEPROM
                                          'at address 32
       Pause 10                           'Wait 10 ms for write cycle
                                          'to complete.
       address = 33
       I2cout control, address, (21)
       Pause 10
```

If..Then

```
If Comp Then Label
```

This command performs a comparison test. If the particular condition is met (is true), then the program execution jumps to the statements beginning at

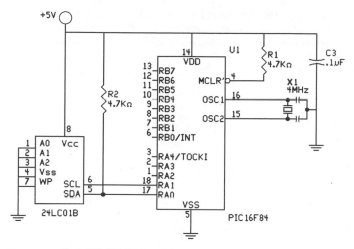

Figure 5.2 Serial EEPROM interface.

Label. If the condition is not true, program execution continues at the next line.

The Then in the If..Then is essentially a Goto. Another statement cannot be placed after the Then; what follows must be a label.

The command compares variables to constants or to other variables. If only one variable is used in a comparison, it must be placed on the left. All comparisons are unsigned.

The following is a list of valid comparisons:

=	Equal to
<	Greater than
>	Less than
<>	Not equal to
<=	Less than or equal to
>=	Greater than or equal to

```
If B8 <= 25 Then loop
```

If the value in variable B8 is less than or equal to 25, then the program jumps to loop.

Binary logic comparisons

The If..Then command may also be used with two binary logic comparisons, AND and OR.

Input

```
Input Pin
```

This command makes the specified pin an input pin. Only the pin number itself, 0 to 7, is specified in the command. The command works only on port B pins.

```
Input 1            'Make pin 1 (RB1) an input.
```

Let

```
Let Var = Value
```

Optional:

```
Where Value = OP Value
```

Let assigns a value to a variable.
  The value assigned may be

1. A constant (Let B1 = 27)
2. The value of another variable (Lct B1 − B2)
3. The result of one or more binary (math) operations

The operations are performed strictly left to right and all operations are performed with 16-bit precision.
  Valid operations are

+	Addition
-	Subtraction
*	Multiplication
**	Most significant bit of multiplication
/	Division
//	Remainder
MIN	Minimum
MAX	Maximum
&	Bitwise AND
:	Bitwise OR
^	Bitwise XOR
& /	Bitwise AND NOT
: /	Bitwise OR NOT
^ /	Bitwise XOR NOT

Sample operations:

```
Let B1 = 34        'Assign variable B1 the value of 34 ("Let" is optional)
Let B1 = B0 / 2    'Assign variable B1 to B0's value shifted right one bit
                   '(divided by 2)
```

When two 16-bit numbers are multiplied, the result used is the lower 16 bits of the 32-bit answer.

```
Let W1 = W0 * 256          'Multiply value held in W0 by 256 and
                           'place result in W1 (lower 16 bits)
```

If you require the higher-order 16 bits, use the following command:

```
Let W1 = W0 ** 256         'Multiply value held in W0 by 256 and
                           'place result in W1 (upper 16 bits)
```

Bitwise operations use standard binary logic and 8-bit bytes.

```
B1 = %01100000
B2 = %00100010
Let B2 = B2 & B1
```

The resultant B2 will be %00100000.

Lookdown

```
Lookdown Svalue, (cvalue0, cvalue1,...,cvalueN), rvalue
```

where svalue = search value
     cvalueX = constant values
     rvalue = result value

The Lookdown command searches through a list of constants (*cvalue0*, *cvalue1*, etc.), comparing each value in the list to the search value (*Svalue*). If a match is found, the physical number of the term (index number) in the list is stored in the *rvalue* (result value) variable.

A simple example will straighten out any confusion.

```
Lookdown 5, ("16, 34, 21, 13, 7  8  9, 10, 5 2"), B0
```

The command searches through the list of constants and stores the item number in B0. In this example, B0 will hold the result of 8. (Lookdown begins counting from 0, not 1.) Commas are used to delineate multiple-digit numbers.

The constant list may be a mixture of numeric and string constants. Each character in a string is treated as a separate constant with the character's ASCII value.

If the search value is not in the lookdown list, no action is taken and the value of *rvalue* remains unchanged.

ASCII values as well as numeric values may be searched.

```
Serin 1, N2400,B0          'Get hexadecimal character from pin 1 serially
Lookdown B0, ("0123456789ABCDEF"), B1
                           'Convert hexadecimal character in B0 to
                           'decimal value in B1.
Serout 0,N2400, (#B1)      'Send decimal value to pin 0 serially.
```

Lookup

```
Lookup Index, (cvalue0, cvalue1,...,(cvalueN), Value
```

The Lookup command is used to retrieve values from a table of constants (*cvalue0*, *cvalue1*, etc.). The retrieved value is stored in the *Value* variable. If the index is zero, *Value* is set to the value of *cvalue0*. If the index is set to 1, then *Value* is set to the value of *cvalue1*, and so on.

If the index number is greater than the number of constants available to read, no action is taken and *Value* remains unchanged.

The constant may be numbers or string constants. Each character in a string is treated as a separate constant equal to the character's ASCII value.

```
For B0 = 0 to 5              'Set up For..Next loop*p900X
Lookup B0, ("Hello!")        'Get character number B0 from
                             'string and place in variable B1
        Serout 0,N2400, (B1) 'Send character in B1 out on pin 0
                             'serially.
Next B0                      'Do next character.
```

Low

```
Low Pin
```

This command makes the specified pin an output pin and brings it low (0 V). Only the pin number itself, 0 to 7, is specified in the command. The command works only on port B pins.

```
Low 0        'Make pin 0 (RB0) an output pin and bring it low
             ' ( 0 V )
```

Nap

```
Nap Period
```

This command places the PIC microcontroller in low-power mode for varying short periods of time. During a Nap, power consumption is reduced to a minimum. The following table of times is approximate, because the timing cycle is derived from the on-board watchdog timer, which is *R/C* driven and varies from chip to chip (and with temperature).

Period	Delay (approximate)
0	18 ms
1	36 ms
2	72 ms
3	144 ms
4	288 ms
5	576 ms
6	1.15 s
7	2.3 s

```
Nap 7        'Low-power pause for 2.3 s
```

The watchdog timer must be enabled in the EPIC software (see EPIC Software) for Nap and Sleep commands to function. If Nap and Sleep commands are not used, the watchdog timer may be disabled.

Output

```
Output Pin
```

This command makes the specified pin an output pin. Only the pin number itself, 0 to 7, is specified in the command. The command works only on port B pins.

```
Output 5       'Make pin 5 (RB5) an output.
```

Pause

```
Pause Period
```

This command provides a pause in program execution for the *Period* in milliseconds. *Period* is a 16-bit number that can hold a maximum value of 65,535. In milliseconds, that works out to just over one minute (60,000 ms). Unlike the other delay functions, Nap and Sleep, the Pause command does not put the microcontroller into a low-power mode. This has both an advantage and a disadvantage. The disadvantage is that Pause consumes more power; the advantage is that the clock is more accurate.

```
Pause 250        'Delay for 1/4 s
```

Peek

```
Peek Address, Variable
```

The Peek command reads any of the microcontroller's registers at the *Address* specified and copies the result in *Var*. This command may be used to read special registers such as A/D converters and additional I/O ports.

Peek reads the entire 8 bits of the register at once. If extensive bit manipulation is needed, the user may store the results of the Peek command in either B0 or B1. These two bytes may be also be used as bit variables Bit0 to Bit15, and extensive bit manipulation is easily performed. Byte B0 is equivalent to Bit0 to Bit7, and byte B1 is equivalent to Bit8 to Bit15.

The following example shows how one can check bit status. It assumes that the five open pins on port A have been configured as input pins.

```
loop:
      Peek PortA, B0           'Read port A pins and copy result
                               'into byte B0.
      If Bit0 = 1 Then route1  'If RA0 is high, jump to route1
      If Bit1 = 1 Then route2  'If RA1 is high, jump to route2
      If Bit2 = 1 Then route3  'If RA3 is high, jump to route3
```

```
        If Bit3 = 0 Then route1   'If RA4 is low, jump to route1
        If Bit4 = 0 Then route1   'If RA5 is low, jump to route2
Goto loop
```

The example shows that bits may be checked for high or low status. The Peek command also works with pins that are configured as outputs. When peeked, the resultant shows the binary value that has been poked in the port register.

Poke

```
Poke Address, Variable
```

The Poke command can write to any of the microcontroller's registers at the *Address* specified and copy the value in *Var* to the register. This command may be used to write to special registers such as A/D converters and additional I/O ports.

Poke writes an entire byte (8 bits) to the register at once.

```
Poke 134,0     'Write binary 0 to DDR for port B, making all pins
               'output lines..
```

Pot

```
Pot Pin, Scale, Var
```

This command reads a potentiometer or other resistive transducer on the *Pin* specified. The programmer may choose any of the port B pins, 0 to 7, to use with this command.

Resistance is measured by timing the discharge of a capacitor through the resistor, usually 5 to 50 kΩ. *Scale* is used to adjust varying *R/C* constants. For large *R/C* constants, set *Scale* to 1. For small *R/C* constants, set *Scale* to its maximum value of 255. Ideally, if *Scale* is set correctly, the variable *Var* will be set to zero at minimum resistance and to 255 at maximum resistance.

Scale must be determined experimentally. Set the device or transducer to measure at maximum resistance and read it with *Scale* set to 255. Under these conditions, *Var* will produce an approximate value for *Scale*.

There are many resistive-type transducers that may be read using the Pot command. The important thing that distinguishes this command from an analog-to-digital (A/D) converter is that a converter measures voltage, not resistance. [Although the voltage drop across the converter may seem to be similar to the Pot diagram (Fig. 5.3), it is not.]

```
Pot 3,255,B0              'Read potentiometer on pin 3 to
                          'determine scale.
Serout 0,N2400, (#B0)     'Send pot values out on pin 0
                          'serially.
```

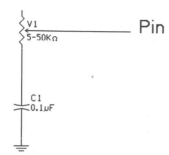

Figure 5.3 Pot command test circuit.

Pulsin

```
Pulsin Pin, State, Var
```

This command measures the pulse width in 10-μs increments on the *Pin* specified. If *State* is 0, the width of the low portion of the pulse is measured. If *State* is 1, the width of the high portion of the pulse is measured. The measured width is stored in variable *Var*. The variable *Var* is a 16-bit number and therefore can contain numbers from 0 to 65,535. To calculate the measured pulse width, multiple *Var* by 10 μs.

$$Var * 10 \ \mu s = measured \ pulse \ width$$

Pulse widths from 10 to 655,350 μs can be measured.

If the pulse width is larger than the maximum width the microcontroller can measure, *Var* is set to zero. If an 8-bit variable is used for *Var*, only the lower byte (LSB) of the 16-bit measurement is stored. This command may use any port B pin from 0 to 7.

```
Pulsin 2,0,W2     'Measure low pulse on pin 2 (RB2) and
                  'place width measurement * 10 μs in
                  'W2
```

Pulsout

```
Pulsout Pin, Period
```

This command generates a pulse on the *Pin* specified. The pulse width is specified by *Period*. The variable *Period* is a 16-bit number that can range from 0 to 65,535. The pulse width is calculated by multiplying the variable *Period* by 10 μs.

$$Period * 10 \ \mu s = pulse \ width$$

Therefore, pulse widths from 10 to 655,350 μs may be generated.

Pulses are generated by toggling the pin twice. Thus, the initial state of the pin, 0 or 1, determines the polarity of the pulse.

As a result, if the initial state of the pin is low, Pulsout outputs a positive pulse. On the other hand, if the initial state of the pin is high (+5 V), Pulsout outputs a negative (0 V) pulse. This command may use any port B pin from 0 to 7. The pin used is automatically made into an output pin.

```
Low 6                    'Set pin 6 (RB6) to an output and bring it
                         'low
Pulsout 6,1000           'Send a positive pulse 10,000 µs (10
                         'ms) long out on pin 6 (RB6).
```

Pwm

```
Pwm Pin, Duty, Cycle
```

This command outputs a pulse-width-modulation (PWM) train on the *Pin* specified. Each cycle of PWM consists of 256 steps. The *Duty* cycle for each PWM ranges from 0 (0 percent) to 255 (100 percent). This PWM cycle is repeated *Cycle* times. This command may use any port B pin from 0 to 7.

The pin is made an output just prior to pulse generation and reverts to an input after generation stops. This allows a simple *R/C* circuit to be used as a simple D/A converter.

The test circuit for this command is shown in Fig. 5.4.

```
Pwm 7,126,155    'Send a 50 percent duty cycle PWM signal out on
                 'pin 7 (RB7) for 155 cycles.
```

Note: If the PWM command is used to control a high-current device, the output signal should be buffered.

Random

```
Random Var
```

This command generates a pseudo-random number in *Var*. The variable *Var* must be a 16-bit variable. Random numbers range from 1 to 65,635 (zero is not produced).

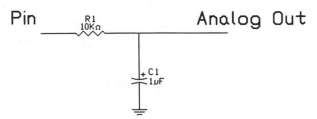

Figure 5.4 PWM test circuit.

```
Random W2           'Generate random number in W2
```

Read

```
Read Address, Var
```

This command reads the on-chip EEPROM (if available) at the specified *Address*; the resultant byte at the address is copied into the *Var* variable. If *Address* is 255, *Var* returns with the number of EEPROM bytes available. This instruction may be used only with microcontrollers that contain on-chip EEP-ROM, such as the 16F84.

```
Read 5, B0          'Read EEPROM location number 5 and copy
                    'into B0.
```

Return

```
Return
```

This command causes program execution to return from a called Gosub command.

```
Gosub send1                     'Jump to subroutine labeled send1
...                             'Program returns here
...
' ' '
send1:                          'Subroutine send1 begins
Serout 0,N2400, ("Hello!")      'Send "Hello!" out on pin 0 serially
Return                          'Return to main program
```

Reverse

```
Reverse Pin
```

This command reverses the status of the *Pin* specified. If *Pin* is an output, it is reversed to an input, and vice versa. Only the pin number itself, 0 to 7, is specified in the command. The command works only on port B pins.

```
Output 3    'Make pin 3 (RB3) an output pin
Reverse 3   'Change pin 3 (RB3) to an input pin
```

Serin

```
Serin Pin, Mode, [ (Qual { ,Qual } ), ] Item { ,Item }
```

This command allows the microcontroller to receive serial data on the *Pin* specified. The data are received in standard asynchronous mode using 8 data bits, no parity bit, and 1 stop bit. *Mode* sets the baud rate and TTL polarity as follows:

Symbol	Baud rate	Polarity
T2400	2400	TTL true
T1200	1200	TTL true
T9600	9600	TTL true
T300	300	TTL true
N2400	2400	TTL inverted
N1200	1200	TTL inverted
N9600	9600	TTL inverted
N300	300	TTL inverted

The operation of this command is shown in Fig. 5.5.

```
'Convert decimal number to hexadecimal
Loop:
Serin 1, N2400, B0                          'Receive decimal
                                            'number on pin 1, 2400
                                            'Baud; store in B0.

Lookup B0, ("0123456789ABCDEF"), B1         'Use B0 as index
                                            'number and look up
                                            'hex equivalent.

Serout 0, N2400, (B1, 13, 10)               'Transmit hex
                                            'equivalent out on pin 0
                                            'serially with carriage
                                            'return (13) and line
                                            'feed (10).

Goto Loop                                   'Do it again.
```

Triggers

The microcontroller can be configured to ignore all serial data until a particular byte or sequence of bytes is received. This byte or sequence of bytes is called a qualifier and is enclosed within parentheses. If there is more than one byte in a qualifier, Serin must receive these bytes in exact order before receiving data. If a byte does not match the next byte in a qualifying sequence, the qualification process resets. If this happens, the next byte received is compared to the first item in the qualification sequence. Once the qualification is met, Serin begins receiving data.

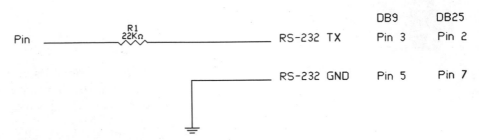

Figure 5.5 Serial in from RS-232.

The qualifier can be a constant, variable, or string. Each character of a string is treated as an individual qualifier.

```
Serin 1, N2400, ("A"), B0
```

Wait until the character "A" is received serially on pin 1, then put the next character in B0.

Serout

```
Serout Pin, Mode, Item {,Item}
```

This command allows the microcontroller to transmit serial data on the *Pin* specified. The data are transmitted in standard asynchronous mode using 8 data bits, no parity bit, and 1 stop bit. *Mode* sets the baud rate and TTL polarity as follows:

Symbol	Baud rate	Polarity
T2400	2400	TTL true
T1200	1200	TTL true
T9600	9600	TTL true
T300	300	TTL true
N2400	2400	TTL inverted
N1200	1200	TTL inverted
N9600	9600	TTL inverted
N300	300	TTL inverted
OT2400	2400	Open drain
OT1200	1200	Open drain
OT9600	9600	Open drain
OT300	300	Open drain
ON2400	2400	Open source
ON1200	1200	Open source
ON9600	9600	Open source
ON300	300	Open source

Serout supports three types of data, which may be mixed and matched freely within a single Serout statement. A description of the data types follows:

1. A string constant is transmitted as a literal string of characters.

2. A numeric value (either a variable or a constant) will transmit the corresponding ASCII character. This procedure is often used to transmit a carriage return (13) and a line feed (10).

3. A numeric value preceded by a pound sign (#) will transmit as the ASCII representation of its decimal value. For instance, if W0 = 123, then #W0 (or #123) will transmit as "1", "2", "3".

The operation of this command is shown in Fig. 5.6.

```
Serout 0,N2400, (#B0,10)   'Send the ASCII value of B0 followed by
                           'a line feed out pin 0 serially.
```

Note: Single-chip RS-232-level converters are common and inexpensive (Maxim's MAX232) and should be implemented when needed or to ensure proper RS-232 communication.

Sleep

```
Sleep Period
```

This command places the microcontroller in low power mode for *Period*, specified in seconds. Since *Period* is a 16-bit number, delays of up to 65,535 s (a little over 18 h) are possible. Sleep uses the watchdog timer (WDT) on the microcontroller, which has a resolution of 2.3 s (see Nap command).

```
Sleep 120       'Sleep (low-power mode) for 2 min.
```

Additional sleep notes

It has been determined that Sleep may not work properly on all PICMicros. During Sleep calibration, the PICMicro is reset. Different devices respond in different ways to this reset. Upon reset, many registers may be altered. Notably the TRIS registers set all the port pins to inputs.

However the TRIS register for port B is automatically saved and restored by the Sleep routine. Any other port directions must be reset by the user program after Sleep. Other registers may also be affected. See the data sheets for a particular part for this information.

To get around potential problems, an uncalibrated version of Sleep has been added. This version does not cause a device reset, so it has no effect on any of the internal registers. All the registers, including port direction, remain unchanged during and after a Sleep instruction.

However, actual Sleep times will no longer be as accurate and will vary, depending on device particulars and temperature. To enable the uncalibrated version of Sleep, add the following lines to a PBC program:

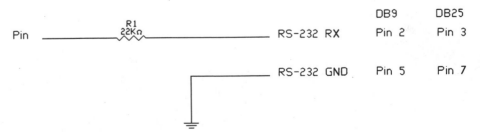

Figure 5.6 Serial out to RS-232.

```
asm
SLEEPUNCAL = 1
endasm
```

The PICBasic Compiler software is packaged with a PICMicro macro assembler (PM.exe). While we will not write any in-line assembly code, it is available to those who have some familiarity with assembly language and PBC library routines. The next book will mix assembly and Basic language and use the PICMicro macro assembler.

Sound

```
Sound Pin, ( Note, Duration {, Note, Duration} )
```

This command generates tones and/or white noise on the specified *Pin*. Note 0 is silence, notes 1 to 127 are tones, and notes 128 to 255 are white noise. Tones and white noises are in ascending order. *Duration* is a numeric variable from 0 to 255 that determines how long the specified note is played. Each increment in duration is equivalent to approximately 12 ms. This command may use any port B pin from 0 to 7.

The waveform output is TTL level square waves. A small speaker and capacitor can be driven directly from the microcontroller pin (see Fig. 5.7). Piezo speakers may be driven directly.

```
Sound 4, (100,10,50,10)     'Play two notes consecutively on pin 4
                            '(RB4).
```

Toggle

```
Toggle Pin
```

This command inverts the state of the specified *Pin*. The pin specified is automatically made into an output pin. This command may use any port B pin from 0 to 7.

```
High 1          'Make pin 1 (RB1) high
Toggle 1        'Invert state of pin 1 and bring it low
```

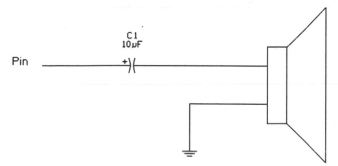

Figure 5.7 Simple sound out circuit.

Write

```
Write Address, Value
```

This command writes the *Value* to the on-chip EEPROM (if available) at the specified *Address*. This instruction may be used only with microcontrollers that contain on-chip EEPROM, such as the 16F84.

```
Write 5,B0       ' Write the value in B0 to EEPROM address 5
```

6

Characteristics of the I6F84 Microcontroller

In this chapter, we will look at a few aspects of our PIC 16F84 microcontroller.

Current Maximums for I/O Port(s)

Maximum output current sourced by any I/O pin	20 mA
Maximum input current sunk by any I/O pin	25 mA
Maximum current sourced by port A	50 mA
Maximum current sunk by port A	80 mA
Maximum current sourced by port B	100 mA
Maximum current sunk by port B	150 mA
Typical operating current	1.8 mA

Other factors such as I/O pin loading, operating voltage, and frequency have an impact on the operating current.

Power-down current in Sleep mode (I/O pins' high-impedance state)   7 μA

Clock Oscillators

PIC microcontrollers can be operated in four different oscillator modes. We select the oscillator mode when we program the microcontroller using the EPIC software. We have the option of selecting one of the following modes:

LP   Low-power crystal
XT   Crystal/resonator
HS   High-speed crystal/resonator
RC   Resistor/capacitor

In the XT, LP, or HS mode, a crystal or ceramic resonator is connected to the OCS1/CLKIN and OSC2/CLKOUT pins to establish oscillation (see Fig. 6.1). For crystals 2.0 to 10.0 MHz, the recommended capacitance for C1 and C2 is in the range of 15 to 33 pF. Crystals provide accurate timing to within ±50 ppm (parts per million). For a 4-MHz crystal, this works out to ±200 Hz.

A ceramic resonator with built-in capacitors is a three-terminal device that is connected as shown in Fig. 6.2. The timing accuracy of resonators is approximately ±0.5 percent. For a 4-MHz resonator, this works out to ±20,000 Hz.

RC oscillators may be implemented with a resistor and a capacitor (see Fig. 6.3). While additional cost saving is provided, applications using *RC* mode must be insensitive to timing. In other words, it would be hard to establish RS-232 serial communication using an *RC* oscillator because of the variance in component tolerances.

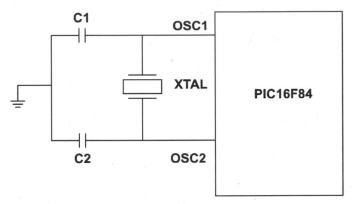

Figure 6.1 Crystal connected to PIC 16F84.

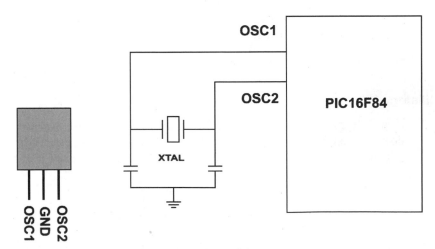

Figure 6.2 Diagram of ceramic resonator with built-in capacitors.

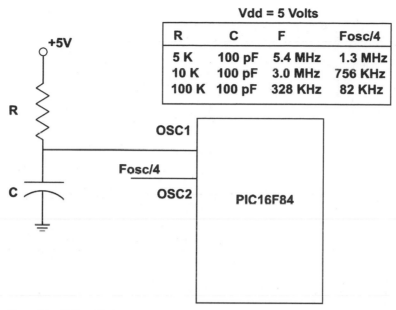

Figure 6.3 *RC* oscillator.

To ensure maximum stability with *RC* oscillators, Microchip recommends keeping the *R* value between 5 and 100 kΩ. The capacitor value should be greater than 20 pF.

There is not a standard formula for calculating the *RC* values needed for a particular frequency. Microchip provides this information in the form of graphs given in the data sheets for particular microcontrollers.

The *RC* oscillator frequency, divided by 4, is available on the OSC2/CLK-OUT pin. This output can be used for testing and as a clock signal to synchronize other components.

An external clock may also be used in the XT, LP, and HS modes. External clocks require only a connection to the OSC1 pin (see Fig. 6.4). This is useful when we are attempting to design an entire circuit that can be implemented with one external clock for all components. Clock accuracy is typically similar to the accuracy quoted for crystals.

Reset

The PIC 16F84 can differentiate between different kinds of resets. During reset, most registers are placed in an unknown condition or a "reset state." The exception to this is a watchdog timer (WDT) reset during Sleep, because the PICBasic compiler automatically stores TRISB register when using the Sleep command and reinitializes TRISB after a reset for the resumption of normal operation. The following types of resets are possible:

Power-on reset

MCLR reset during normal operation

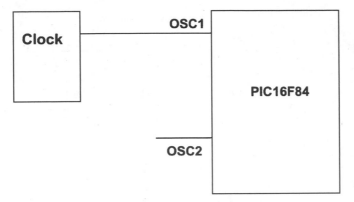

Figure 0.4 External clock.

MCLR reset during Sleep

WDT reset during normal operation

WDT wake-up (during Sleep)

For the time being, we are concerning ourselves only with the MCLR reset during normal operation. The MCLR pin is kept high for normal operation. In the event that it is necessary to reset the microcontroller, bring the MCLR pin momentarily low (see Fig. 6.5).

In some cases, you may want to include an optional resistor R2 (100 Ω). This resistor limits any current flowing into MCLR.

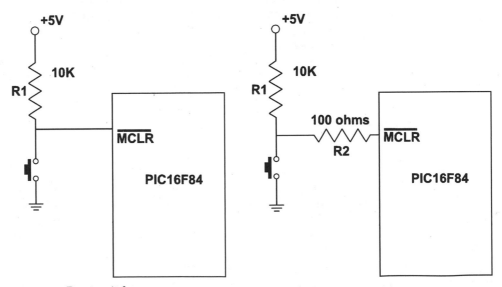

Figure 6.5 Reset switch.

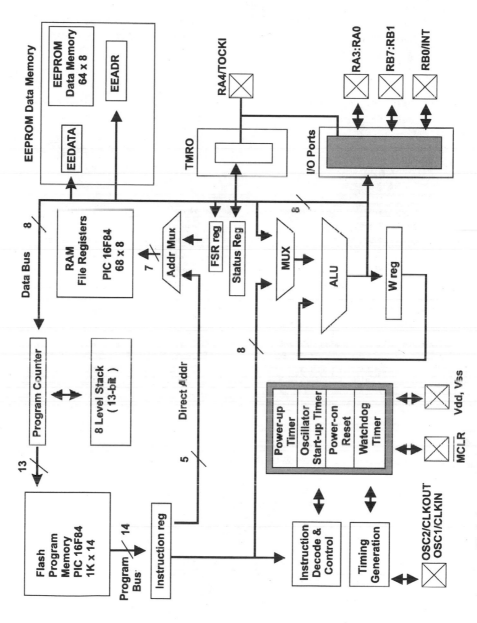

Figure 6.6 Block diagram of the 16F84.

89

PIC Harvard Architecture

PIC microcontrollers use a Harvard architecture, which means that the memory is divided into program memory and data memory. The advantage to this architecture is that both memories can be accessed during the same clock instruction; this makes it faster than the standard von Neumann architecture, which uses a single memory for program and data. Figure 6.6 is a block diagram of the 16F84.

User program memory space extends from 0x0000h to 0x03FFh (0 to 1023 decimal). Accessing a memory space above 03FFh will cause a wraparound to the beginning of the memory space.

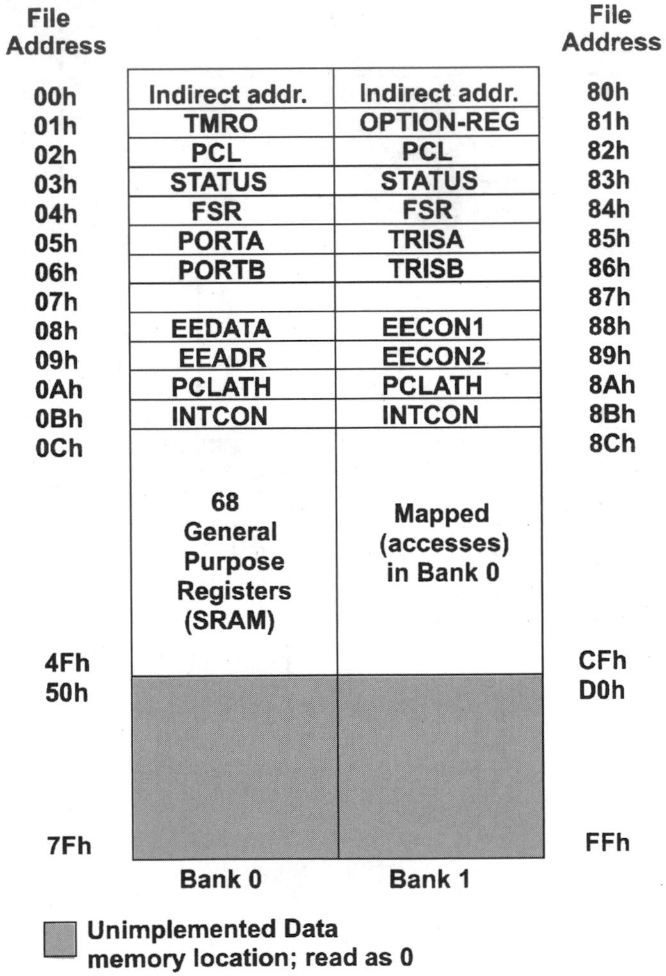

File Address	Bank 0	Bank 1	File Address
00h	Indirect addr.	Indirect addr.	80h
01h	TMRO	OPTION-REG	81h
02h	PCL	PCL	82h
03h	STATUS	STATUS	83h
04h	FSR	FSR	84h
05h	PORTA	TRISA	85h
06h	PORTB	TRISB	86h
07h			87h
08h	EEDATA	EECON1	88h
09h	EEADR	EECON2	89h
0Ah	PCLATH	PCLATH	8Ah
0Bh	INTCON	INTCON	8Bh
0Ch			8Ch
	68 General Purpose Registers (SRAM)	Mapped (accesses) in Bank 0	
4Fh			CFh
50h			D0h
7Fh			FFh

■ Unimplemented Data memory location; read as 0

Figure 6.7 Register file map 16F84.

Register Map

The register map is shown in Fig. 6.7. This memory area is partitioned into two spaces called *banks*. In the diagram you can see the two banks, bank 0 and bank 1. The small *h* behind the numbers under the file address informs us that these are hexadecimal numbers. If you were programming in machine or assembly language, you would have to set a bit in the Status Register to move between the two banks. Fortunately for us, the PICBasic compiler handles this bank switching for us.

There are two addresses I would like to touch upon. The first is the Reset Vector at 00h. Upon power-up or reset, the Program Counter is set to the memory location held at 00.

The Interrupt Vector is shown as FSR 04h. Upon an interrupt, the return address is saved and the program execution continues at the address held in this memory location. On a return from interrupt, the program execution continues at the return address previously saved.

Unfortunately, we do not have time to work with interrupts, watchdog timers, or the Sleep mode in this book. In the next book, we will play with these additional features.

7

Speech Synthesizer

This chapter begins our applications. The first project is a speech synthesizer that can be embedded into another circuit or project to add speech capabilities. You may want to create a talking toaster that will tell you when your toast is ready, or a talking VCR. The circuit is activated and the speech selected by using high or low logic signals to port A.

Speech synthesizers (or processors) are available in two formats. The first format uses sampled (digitally recorded) speech stored in ROM or EEPROM. The second approach uses phonemes of English to construct words. A phoneme is a speech sound.

Each format has its advantages and disadvantages. Digitally recorded speech has excellent fidelity, but has a limited vocabulary because of the large storage capacity required. The phoneme approach has an unlimited vocabulary, but the speech fidelity isn't as good as that of sampled speech. Even so, the phoneme approach usually suffices as long as a mechanical (robotic-type) voice is acceptable. This is the approach we are using.

The total cost of this project, including the PIC microcontroller, should be less than $25.00. Included in this price are an audio amplifier, filter, volume control, and speaker.

While the speech synthesizer chip is capable of producing an unlimited vocabulary, we do not have an unlimited memory in the microcontroller. The limited memory in the microcontroller limits the number of words that can be stored, but they may be any words you want.

In later chapters, we interface serial EEPROMs to the microcontroller; these can be used to increase word vocabulary.

Speech Chip

The SPO-256 speech synthesizer chip we are using was discontinued by General Instruments a number of years ago. However, there is a good supply of chips available from B & S Micro and a few other distributors (see Suppliers

Index). The SPO-256 (see Fig. 7.1) can generate 59 allophones (the electronic equivalent of English phonemes) plus five pauses (no sound) of various lengths. An allophone table is provided in Table 7.1.

By concatenating (adding together) allophones, we construct words and sentences. This may appear difficult at first, but it is not. Once you get the hang of it, you can turn out complete sentences in a minute or so.

A Little on Linguistics

When we program words for the SPO-256 speech chip, we string together the allophones shown in Table 7.1. Words and sentences must end with a pause (silence); if they do not, the last allophone sent to the chip will drone on continuously.

To pronounce the word *cookie*, use the following allophones: cookie = KK3, UH, KK1, IY, PA2. The decimal addresses for the allophones are sent to the SPO-256; this works out to the following numbers: 8, 30, 42, 19, 1.

The optional data sheet for the SPO-256 has an allophone word list containing two hundred or so commonly used words (numbers, months, days of the week, etc.). If the word you need isn't on the list, you can make the word up yourself, using the allophone list.

The first thing to keep in mind when creating an allophone list for any particular word is that there is not a one-to-one correspondence between sounds and letters. You need to spell the words phonetically, using the allophone table. For instance, CAT becomes KAT, which in allophones becomes KK1, EY, TT1,

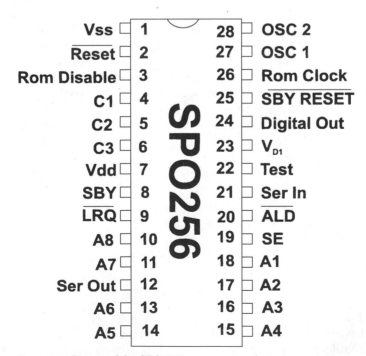

Figure 7.1 Pinout of the SPO-256

TABLE 7.1   Allophones

Decimal address	Allophone	Sample word	Duration (ms)
0	PA1	Pause	10
1	PA2	Pause	30
2	PA3	Pause	50
3	PA4	Pause	100
4	PA5	Pause	200
5	OY	Toy	420
6	AY	Buy	260
7	EH	End	70
8	KK3	Cat	120
9	PP	Power	140
10	JH	Judge	140
11	NN1	Pin	140
12	IH	Sit	70
13	TT2	To	140
14	RR1	Plural	170
15	AX	Succeed	70
16	MM	My	180
17	TT1	Tart	100
18	DH1	They	290
19	IY	Tee	250
20	EY	Beige	280
21	DD1	Should	70
22	UW1	To	100
23	AO	Aught	100
24	AA	Home	100
25	YY2	Yes	180
26	AE	Pat	120
27	HH1	Him	130
28	BB1	Boy	80
29	TH	They	180
30	UH	Book	100
31	UW2	Food	260
32	AW	Out	370
33	DD2	Don't	160
34	GG3	Pig	140
35	VV	Venom	190

(continued)

TABLE 7.1 Allophones *(Continued)*

Decimal address	Allophone	Sample word	Duration (ms)
36	GG1	Gotten	80
37	SH	Sharp	160
38	ZH	Azure	190
39	RR2	Train	120
40	FF	Forward	150
41	KK2	Sky	190
42	KK1	Came	160
43	ZZ	Zolu	210
44	NG	Anchor	220
45	LL	Lamb	110
46	WW	Wood	180
47	XR	Pair	360
48	WH	Whine	200
49	YY1	Yes	130
50	CH	Chump	190
51	ER1	Tire	160
52	ER2	Tire	300
53	OW	Beau	240
54	DH2	They	240
55	SS	Best	90
56	NN2	Not	190
57	HH2	Noe	180
58	OR	Pore	330
59	AR	Arm	290
60	YR	Clear	350
61	GG2	Guide	40
62	EL	Paddle	190
63	BB2	Boy	50

PA1. The decimal addresses for the allophones are 42, 20, 17, 1. Those are the numbers we plug into our program to get it to speak. When the word is programmed in, listen to it as it plays through the SPO-256 and decide whether we need to improve upon it. In our *cat* example, you will find that the KK3 allophone makes the word sound better.

The placement of a speech sound within a word can change its pronunciation. For instance, look at the two *d*'s in the word *depend*. The *d*'s are pronounced differently. The DD2 allophone will sound correct in the first *d* position, and the DD1 allophone will sound correct in the second *d* position.

General Instrument recommends using a 3.12-MHz crystal at pins 27 and 28. I have used a 3.57-MHz TV color burst crystal on many occasions (because of its availability and the unavailability of the 3.12-MHz) without any ill effects. The change increases the timbre of the speech slightly.

Interfacing to the SPO-256

The pinout and functions of the SPO-256 are provided in Table 7.2. The SPO-256 has eight address lines (A1 to A8). In our application, we need to access 64 allophones. Therefore, we need to use only address lines A1 to A6. The two other address lines, A7 and A8, are tied to ground (0). Thus, any access to the SPO-256 address bus will include the address we place on A1 to A6, with lines A7 and A8 = 0. Essentially, A7 and A8 add nothing to the address.

TABLE 7.2 SPO-256 Pin Functions

Pin number	Name	Function
1	Vss	Ground
2	Reset	Logic 0, reset
		Logic 1, normal operation
3	ROM disable	Used with external serial ROM. Logic 1 disables
4, 5, 6	C1, C2, C3	Output control lines for use with serial ROM
7	Vdd	Power (+5 V dc)
8	SBY	Standby
		Logic 1, inactive
		Logic 0, active
9	LRQ	Load request
		Logic 1, active
		Logic 0, inactive
10, 11, 13, 14, 15, 16, 17, 18	A8, A7, A6, A5, A4, A3, A2, A1	Address lines
12	Ser Out	Serial address out. For use with serial ROM
19	SE	Strobe enable. Normally set to logic 1 (mode 1)
20	ALD	Address load. Negative pulse loads address into port
21	Ser In	Serial in. For use with serial ROM
22	Test	Grounded for normal operation
23	Vd1	+ 5 V dc for interface logic
24	Digital Out	Digital speech output
25	SBY Reset	Standby reset. Logic 0 resets
26	ROM clock	1.56-MHz clock output for use with serial ROM
27	OSC1	Crystal in. 3.12 MHz
28	OSC2	Crystal out. 3.12 MHz

Mode Select

There are two modes available for accessing the chip. Mode 0 (SE = 0) will latch an address whenever any of the address pins makes a low-to-high transition. You can think of this as an asynchronous mode.

Mode 1 (SE = 1) latches an address using the ALD pin. When the ALD pin is pulsed low, any address on the lines is latched in. To ensure proper synchronization, there are two pins that can tell the microcontroller when the SPO-256 is ready to have the next allophone address loaded. We will use one of those pins, called the SBY pin. The SBY goes high while the chip is enunciating the allophone. As soon as the allophone is completed, the SBY line goes low. This signals the microprocessor to load the next allophone address on lines A1 to A6 and pulse the ALD line low.

The Circuit

The circuit is shown in Fig. 7.2. The circuit uses two switches to trigger speech. It is important to realize that the switches provide digital logic signals to the port A pins and, further, that any circuit that can output binary 0s and 1s can be used to trigger the circuit to speak. In other words, you don't need to use switches.

Looking at the schematic, we can see that the RA0 and RA1 lines are normally kept high (+5 V), binary 1, through the 10-kΩ resistor. When a switch is closed, it connects the pin to ground and the line is brought down to (ground) binary 0. I could have arranged the logic signals to the pin(s) to be the opposite. This would change a few commands in the program, but functionally it would do the same thing. You choose the logic signal to use based upon the circuit you are working with.

The other important thing to know is that the five open lines on port A may be used to trigger up to 31 different speech announcements. The five pins form a 5-bit binary number that can be read with the Peek command. This is hinted at in the program. We use only two of the five available lines, RA0 and RA1, to jump to three different words. With a 2-bit number, we have four possible combinations.

Logic status

RA0	RA1	Action
1	1	None—normal state
1	0	Speak word 1
0	1	Speak word 2
0	0	Speak word 3

In a similar fashion, a 3-bit number allows 8 unique combinations, a 4-bit number allows 16, and a 5-bit number allows 31.

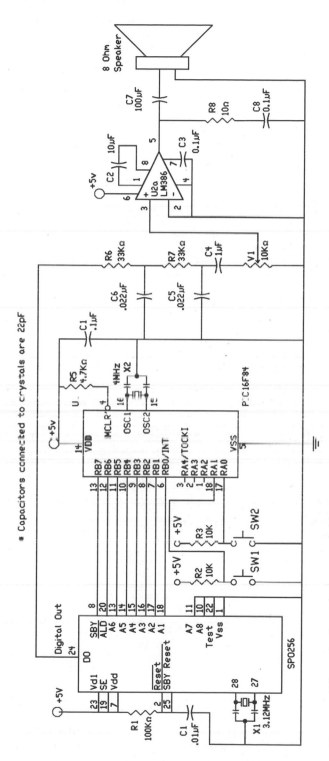

Figure 7.2 Schematic of speech generator circuit.

In the program, word 3 is actually a sentence. This simply demonstrates that you are not limited to using single words.

The Program

```
'REM SPO-256 talker
Symbol TRISB = 134
Symbol portB = 6
Symbol portA = 5
'Initialize ports
Poke TRISB,128              ' Set RB7 as input, set RB0 to RB6 as outputs
'Check line status          ' Could be switches or could be TTL logic signals
start:
Pause 200                   ' Give a human a chance to press a button(s)
Peek portA,b0               ' Read Port A
If b0 = 0 Then three        'Check both lines first (normally b0 = 3)
If bit0 = 0 Then hello      'Check line 0 / alternative command: If b0 = 2
If bit1 = 0 Then world      'Check line 1 / alternative command: If b0 = 1
Goto start
'
'Say word hello
hello:                                 'It's not just a word, it's a routine
For b3 = 0 to 5                        'Loop using number of allophones
lookup b3,(27,7,45,15,53,1),b4        'Decimal addresses of allophones
Gosub speak                            'Speak subroutine
Next b3                                'Get next allophone
Goto start                            'Do it again from the beginning
'
'Say word world
world:                                 'Procedure similar to hello
For b3 = 0 to 4
lookup b3,(46,58,62,21,1),b4
Gosub speak
Next b3
Goto start
'
'Say sentence 'See you next Tuesday.'
three:                                 'Procedure similar to Hello
For b3 = 0 to 19
lookup b3,(55,55,19,1,49,22,1,11,7,42,55,13,2,13,31,43,2,33,20,1),b4
Gosub speak
Next b3
Goto start
'
speak:                      'Subroutine to speak allophones
Poke portB,b4              'Set up allophone address and bring ALD low
Pause 1                    'Pause 1 ms for everything to stabilize
High 6                     'Bring ALD high / alternative: Poke portB, 64
wait:
Peek portB,b0             'Look at port B
If bit7 = 0 Then wait     'Check SBY line (0 = talking, 1 = finished)
Return                    'Get next allophone
```

Program Features

Usually each program has a little something different from all the other programs we looked at so far, and this program is no exception.

Starting from the top, notice how we are using the Peek command:

```
Peek portA, b0
```

First, we are peeking port A, where our two switches are connected, and placing the result in variable b0. If neither switch is pressed, there is a logic high (+5 V) on pins RA0 and RA1. In binary, this port looks like XXX00011, where each X means that the line (pin) is not available for use (read these pins as 0). Following the Xs are the binary 0s equal to pins RA4, RA3, and RA2, and finally the binary 1s equal to pins RA1 and RA0. The decimal equivalent of this binary number is 3. If you have forgotten how to read binary numbers, look back to Table 3.1.

The program interprets this information two ways. First, it looks at the number itself:

```
If b0 = 0 Then three
```

The only way b0 can be zero is if both switches are closed simultaneously. In that case, the program jumps to the routine labeled three. Otherwise, the program continues to the next line.

```
If bit0 = 0 Then hello
```

In this line, we are testing the bit 0 value in the b0 byte. This operation can be performed only on bytes being held in the b0 and b1 variables. In general, try to leave these two variables alone and use them for bit access. In the event that these variables are not available, there are alternative commands that you can use, such as those given in the comments as alternative commands.

```
If bit0 = 0 Then hello   'Check line 0 / alternative command: If b0  a
```

The alternative command may be used on any variable (b7, for instance). I used shorthand for the alternative command to make it fit on one line; the full command would look like this:

```
If b0 = 2 Then hello
```

This checks the number held in the variable. If bit 1 is high, the value of b0 is 2. The disadvantage is that you must keep the status of the other bits in mind when you are checking status in this way.

The Lookup commands are reading numbers rather than ASCII codes. To read numbers, leave out the quotation marks after the parenthesis. ASCII codes use the quotation marks, as in "H."

In the speak subroutine near the end of the program, we use the Peek command again, this time to look at the one input line on port B, the RB7 line. Notice, however, that we peek the entire port B (8 bits), even though there is only one input line. The I/O status of any line doesn't affect the usability of the Peek command. When we peek an output line (or port), the result shows us the status of both the output line(s) and the input lines. After we peek port B, we are checking the status of the one input line RB7 using the bit7 command.

The input line RB7 is connected to the SBY line of the SPO-256. The SBY line stays low while the chip is talking; when it finishes, the line goes high. This tells the PIC microcontroller that it is ready for the next allophone. While the chip is talking, with the SBY line low, the program holds in a waiting loop until SBY goes high.

This is also the first program that uses Gosub routines. In general, it is recommended that you not nest more than three Gosub routines; if you do, you stand a good chance of fouling up the stack.

What's a stack? Let's just say it's a pointing register that stores return addresses on top of one another (a stack). The stack holds the addresses arranged in a LIFO (last in, first out) sequence.

Parts List

Components outlined in Chap. 1.

Additional components

(1)	SPO-256 Speech Processor
(1)	8-ohm speaker
(1)	LM386 Audio Amplifier
(1)	10-kΩ potentiometer PC Mount
(3)	0.1-μF capacitors
(2)	0.022 capacitors
(1)	1-μF capacitor
(1)	10-μF capacitor
(1)	100-μF capacitor
(2)	Push-button switches, normally open
(1)	100kΩ resistor, $\frac{1}{4}$-W
(2)	10kΩ resistor, $\frac{1}{4}$-W
(2)	33kΩ resistor, $\frac{1}{4}$-W
(1)	10-Ω resistor, $\frac{1}{4}$-W
(1)	3.12-MHz crystal

Available from: Images Company, James Electronics, JDR MicroDevices, and RadioShack (see Suppliers Index).

8

Serial Communication and Creating I/O Lines

Creating New I/O Ports

The speech generator project from the last chapter demonstrates how quickly a project can gobble up I/O lines. In complex projects, it's easy to run out of I/O lines. So in this little project, we are going to confront this problem head on and see what we can do.

When we run out of I/O lines, our first thought is usually to upgrade to a larger PIC microcontroller, such as the 16F873, which has 22 I/O lines. Eventually, however, regardless of the microcontroller chosen, we run out of I/O lines. So it's to our benefit to learn how to expand existing I/O lines. In this project, we will take two or three I/O lines off port B and expand them to eight output lines. Then we will use three or four I/O lines off port B to create eight input lines. Sounds good? Read on.

Serial Communication

We will use serial communication to expand our I/O lines. Serial communication comes in two flavors, synchronous and asynchronous. Synchronous communication uses a clock line to determine when information on the serial line is valid. Asynchronous communication doesn't use a clock line. In lieu of a clocking line, asynchronous communication requires start and stop bits in conjunction with strict adherence to timing protocols for its serial communication to be successful.

We use synchronous communication with a clocking line in these projects.

Output First

To create the output lines, we are going to use a serial-to-parallel converter chip, the 74LS164 (see Fig. 8.1). This chip reads 8-bit serial data on pins 1 and 2 and outputs the data on eight parallel lines (QA to QH).

If you remember from the command description of the Basic language (Chap. 5), we have built-in Serin (serial in) and Serout (serial out) commands. Unfortunately, we cannot use these Basic commands because their serial format uses stop and start bits. Start and stop bits are necessary in asynchronous (without a clock) communication.

The 74LS164 converter chips use a clock line and do not use or require stop and start bits. Since there is no way to remove these bits from the standard serial Basic commands, we need to program our own serial communication.

Synchronous communication requires a clocking pulse. The clocking pulse determines when the information on the serial line is valid. For the 74LS164, it is on the low-to-high transition of the clock pulse that information (value 0 or 1) on the serial line is valid.

Basic Serial

Serial data are transmitted most significant bit (bit 7) first. Since we are writing the serial routine, we could change this and send out the least significant bit (bit 0) first if we wanted, but we will not; we will stay with this convention.

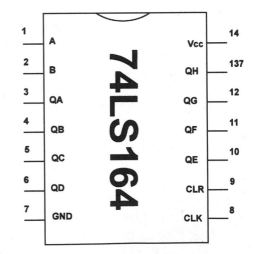

FUNCTION TABLE					
			Outputs		
Clock	A	B	QA	QB ...	QH
X	X	X	L	L ...	L
L	X	X	Qa	Qb ...	Qh
↑	H	H	H	Qa ...	Qg
↑	L	X	L	Qa ...	Qg
↑	X	L	L	Qa ...	Qg

H = high level   L = low level
X = irrelevant (any input including transitions)
↑ = Transition from low to high
Qa ... Qg = the level after the most recent ↑ transition
of the clock; indicates a one bit shift

Figure 8.1   Pinout 74LS164 serial-to-parallel chip.

Figure 8.2 illustrates how the serial data are read by the 74LS164 and parallel information outputted.

Line B (pin 2) on the 74LS164 is kept high. This allows us to use line A (pin 1) to send serial data along with the clocking pulse to pin 8. Notice that in the function table in Fig. 8.1, lines A and B both need to be high for a high bit to be outputted. We can set either line (A or B) high and use the other to transmit serial data; it doesn't matter which we choose.

Each low-to-high transition on the clocking line accepts another bit off line A and outputs that bit to QA. All the existing bit information that is already on the QA to QH lines is shifted 1 bit to the left. After eight transitions, a new 8-bit number is displayed on lines QA to QH of the 74LS164. In Fig. 8.2, we are transmitting binary number 10000000 (decimal number 128). I chose this number so that you can easily see how bit 7, the high bit, shifts down through lines QA to QH.

What isn't immediately evident is that as bit 7 shifts through lines QA to QH, it brings each Qn line high. If we had an LED attached to each Qn line, we could see bit 7 lighting each LED as it shifted with each transition. Only after eight transitions will bit 7 be in the right position. So, after the first seven transitions, as the serial number is shifting into the 74LS164 parallel register, the number shown on the 8-bit parallel output will be incorrect.

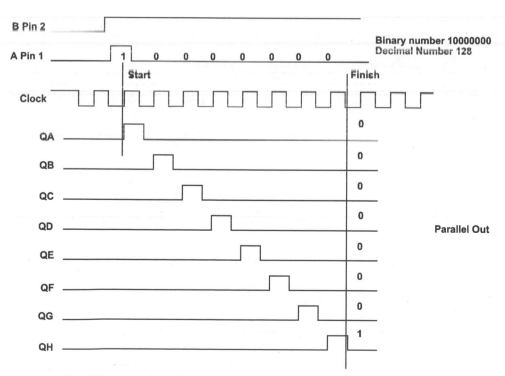

Figure 8.2 Serial data in and parallel data out.

This bit shifting can create chaos in a digital circuit. If the circuit that is connected to the 74LS164 parallel output cannot compensate for this bit shifting, we can correct for this using a second chip, the 74LS373 data octal latch. You will find that some circuits can compensate and others cannot.

Clear Pin

The 74LS164s have an optional pin that can help eliminate some of the havoc caused by bit shifting. Pin 9 on the 74LS164 is the clear (CLR) pin. It is used to clear whatever binary number exists on the parallel output and bring all lines (QA to QH) low. The CLR pin is active low. For normal operation, this pin is kept high. To clear the number, bring the CLR pin low.

The Programs

Program 8.1

```
'Serial interface
'Slow program for visual testing interface
Symbol TRISB = 134  'Assign Data Direction Register port B to 134
Symbol PortB = 6    'Assign variable PortB the decimal value of 6
'Initialize port(s)
Poke TRISB,0        'Set port B as output port
start:
b0 = 128            'Put number 128 (10000000) into b0
Gosub serial        'Output the number serially to 74LS164
Pause 1000          'Wait 1 s
b0 = 255            'Put number 255 (11111111) into b0
Gosub serial        'Output the number serially to 74LS164
Pause 1000          'Wait 1 s
b0 = 0              'Put number 0 (00000000) into b0
Gosub serial        'Output the number serially to 74LS164
Pause 1000          'Wait 1 s
Goto start          'Do it again
'Serial out routine
serial:
pin0 = bit7         'Bring pin 0 high or low, depending upon bit
Pulsout 1, 1        'Bring CLK line high, then low
Pause 100           'Optional delay—remove from program
pin0 = bit6         'Same as above
Pulsout 1, 1        'Same as above
Pause 100           'Optional delay—remove from program
pin0 = bit5
Pulsout 1, 1
Pause 100           'Optional delay—remove from program
pin0 = bit4
Pulsout 1, 1
Pause 100           'Optional delay—remove from program
pin0 = bit3
Pulsout 1, 1
Pause 100           'Optional delay—remove from program
pin0 = bit2
Pulsout 1, 1
Pause 100           'Optional delay—remove from program
pin0 = bit1
Pulsout 1, 1
```

```
Pause 100          'Optional delay—remove from program
pin0 = bit0
Pulsout 1, 1
Pause 100          'Optional delay—remove from program
Low 1
Return
```

The schematic shown in Fig. 8.3 does not correct for the bit shifting. LEDs are connected to the 74LS164 output lines. The program outputs binary 10000000 (decimal 128), waits a second, outputs 11111111 (decimal 255), waits a second, and then outputs 00000000 (decimal 0).

The first serial program has optional Pause commands (Pause 100) after each bit shift to allow you to see how the number shifts into and through the register. These Pause commands should be removed when you are using the serial routine in an application. Remove the Pause command from the program as shown in Program 8.2. Recompile the program and program it into the 16F84. When the program is run, the numbers shift in so quickly that you may not see the bit shifting occurring.

Program 8.2

```
'Serial interface
Symbol TRISB = 134 'Assign Data Direction Register port B to 134
Symbol PortB = 6          'Assign variable PortB the decimal value of 6
'Initialize port(s)
Poke TRISB,0              'Set port B as output port
start:
b0 = 128                 'Put number 128 (10000000) into b0
Gosub serial             'Output the number serially to 74LS164
Pause 1000               'Wait 1 s
b0 = 255                 'Put number 255 (11111111) into b0
Gosub serial             'Output the number serially to 74LS164
Pause 1000               'Wait 1 s
b0 = 0                   'Put number 0 (00000000) into b0
Gosub serial             'Output the number serially to 74LS164
Pause 1000               'Wait 1 s
Goto start               'Do it again
'Serial out routine
serial:
pin0 = bit7              'Bring pin 0 high or low depending upon bit
Pulsout 1, 1             'Bring CLK line high, then low
pin0 = bit6              'Same as above
Pulsout 1, 1             'Same as above
pin0 = bit5
Pulsout 1, 1
pin0 = bit4
Pulsout 1, 1
pin0 = bit3
Pulsout 1, 1
pin0 = bit2
Pulsout 1, 1
pin0 = bit1
Pulsout 1, 1
pin0 = bit0
Pulsout 1, 1
Low 1
Return
```

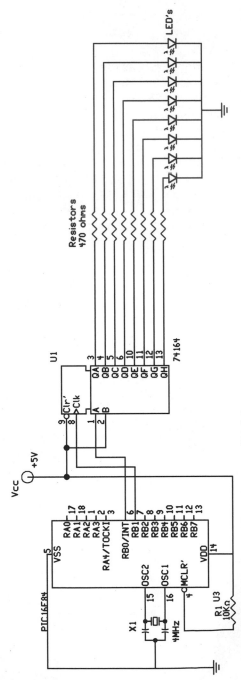

Figure 8.3 Schematic using LEDs to show parallel data output.

BIt Shift Correcting

If you are interfacing to a digital circuit that would be sensitive to the bit shifting, you can block the bit shifting by using a second chip, the 74LS373 data octal latch (see Fig. 8.4). The octal latch is placed between the output of the 74LS164 and the LEDs (see the schematic in Fig. 8.5). Remember, in our testing circuit, the LEDs represent our digital circuit. We tie the OC (Output Enable) pin to ground and use the C (Enable Latch) pin (pin 11 on the 74LS373) to control the data through the 74LS373.

Data are placed on the D inputs (1D, 2D,..., 8D). When we want the data to appear on the Q outputs (1Q, 2Q,..., 8Q), we raise the C pin momentarily.

The program inputs the data serially to the 74LS164. The data appear on the parallel out lines, bit shifting on the inputs of the 74LS373. When the bit shifting is finished and the binary number has settled (eight shifts), we raise the Enable Latch pin (pin 11) of the 74LS373; this lets the parallel data flow from the input pins to the output pins. Then the Enable Latch pin (pin 11) is lowered, leaving the parallel data latched in.

As the bits shift, the bit shifting is blocked from the LEDs. Only when the entire byte has been transmitted do we raise pin 11 (C pin) on the 74LS373,

	74LS373	
1 — $\overline{QC}$		Vcc — 20
2 — 1Q		8Q — 19
3 — 1D		8D — 18
4 — 2D		7D — 17
5 — 2Q		7Q — 16
6 — 3Q		6Q — 15
7 — 3D		6D — 14
8 — 4D		6D — 13
9 — 4Q		5Q — 12
10 — GND		C — 11

FUNCTION TABLE			
Output Enable	Enable Latch	D	Output
L	H	H	H
L	H	L	L
L	L	X	Qo
H	X	X	Z

C = Enable Latch

$\overline{OC}$ = Output Enable

The eight latches of the LS373, when C is high the Q outputs follow the D inputs. When C is low the output will be latched at the current data levels.

Figure 8.4 Octal data latch 74LS373 used to nullify bit shifting in output.

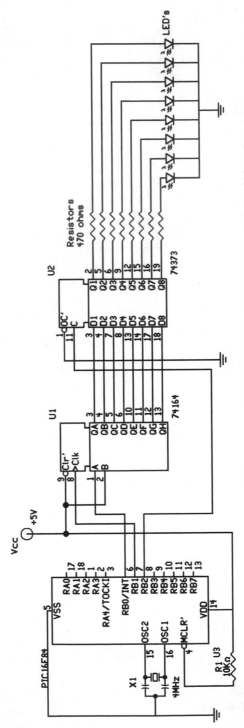

Figure 8.5   Schematic using LEDs to show parallel data output, with 74LS373 data octal latch to nullify bit shifting in output.

letting the byte information through to our LEDs, and then latch in the information.

Programming Challenge (Simple)

Rewrite the first serial program so that pin 2 activates the CLR pin on the 74LS164 to clear the number before loading the next number in. The answer is in the Appendix.

Programming Challenge (Not Simple)

Take the speech generator project from Chap. 7 and use the 74LS164 IC and microcontroller to save four I/O lines and supply the corresponding schematic. *Hint*: You do not need the 74LS373 chip. Why? The answer is in the Appendix.

Input I/O

We shall continue by expanding four I/O lines off the PIC microcontroller to function like eight input lines. To accomplish this, we will use a 74LS165 parallel-to-serial converter chip (see Fig. 8.6). The parallel-in, serial-out diagram is shown in Fig. 8.7. Eight-bit parallel information is placed on the eight input lines of the (A to H) 74LS165. The shift load line is brought low momentarily to load the parallel information into the chip's registers. The

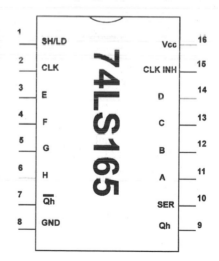

FUNCTION TABLE				
Shift/ Load	Clock	Clock Inhibit	Parallel A .... H	Output Qh
L	X	X	a...h	h
H	L	L	X	Qho
H	↑	L	X	Qgn
H	↑	L	X	Qgn
H	X	H	X	Qho

H = high level   L = low level
X = irrelevant (any input including transitions)
↑ = Transition from low to high

Figure 8.6 Pinout for the 74LS165 parallel-in, serial-out chip.

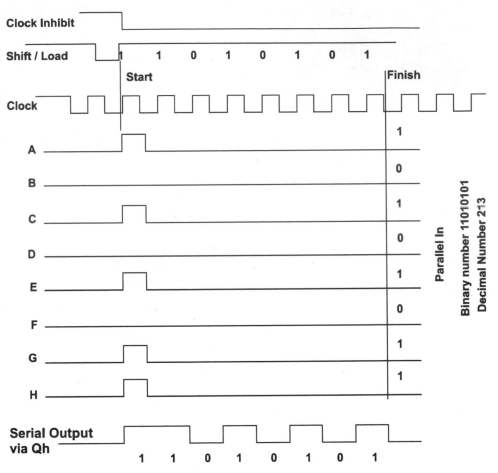

Figure 8.7 Parallel data in and serial data out.

Clock Inhibit line is then brought from high to low, allowing the information to be serially outputted from pin Qh, in synchronization with the clocking pulses provided on pin 2 (CLK). (Note that an inverted serial signal is also available from pin 7.)

To functionally test the chips, circuit, and program, we will input an 8-bit number to the 74LS165 using switches and resistors (see schematic in Fig. 8.8). This binary number created with the switches and resistors will be serially shifted out of the 74LS165 into variable B0. The number in B0 will then be serially sent out to the 74LS164 for display.

We could reduce the number of I/O lines taken up by the 74LS165 by one if we shared the clocking line with the 74LS164. I want to keep the programming as straightforward as possible, so I will not do this, but you should be aware that this feature may be implemented. This would reduce the number of lines required to three.

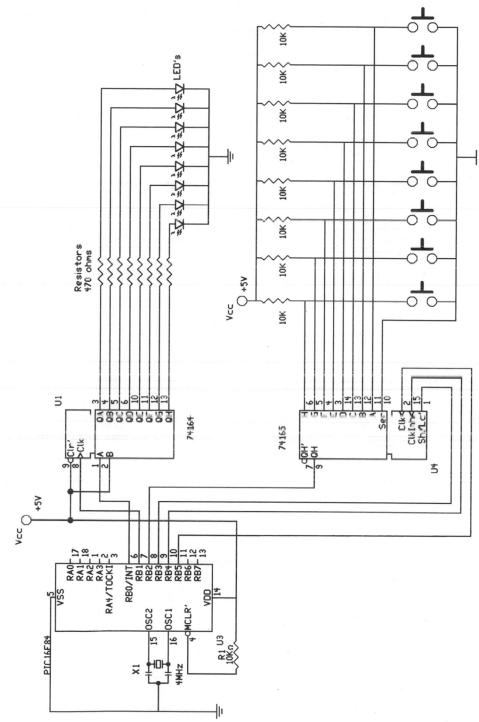

Figure 8.8 Schematic for 74LS164 and 74LS165 serial transmission and receiving.

The serial-out and serial-in routines could be merged to conserve programming space and use the same clocking line. Again, to keep the program as straightforward as possible, this option will not be implemented.

Program 8.3

```
' Serial Interface
Symbol TRISB = 134      'Assign Data Direction Register port B to 134
Symbol PortB = 6        'Assign variable PortB to decimal value of 6
'Initialize Port(s)
Poke TRISB,4            'Set port B Pin2 = input / rest output
Low 5                   'Set CLK low
High 4                  'Bring CLK inhibit high
High 3                  'Bring shift/load high
start:
Gosub serial_in         'Get number from 74LS165
Gosub serial_out        'Send it out on 74LS164
Pause 1000              'Wait so I can see it
Goto start              'Do it again
'Serial In Routine
serial_in:
Pulsout 3,1             'Bring shift / load down momentarily
Low 4                   'Bring CLK inhibit low
bit7 = pin2             'Load bit into B0
Pulsout 5,1             'Bring CLK pin high, then low
bit6 = pin2             'Same as above
Pulsout 5,1
bit5 = pin2
Pulsout 5,1
bit4 = pin2
Pulsout 5,1
bit3 = pin2
Pulsout 5,1
bit2 = pin2
Pulsout 5,1
bit1 = pin2
Pulsout 5,1
bit0 = pin2
High 4                  'Bring CLK inhibit high
Return
'Serial Out Routine
serial_out:
pin0 = bit7             'Bring pin0 high or low depending upon bit
Pulsout 1, 1            'Bring CLK line low, then high
pin0 = bit6             'Same as above
Pulsout 1, 1            'Same as above
pin0 = bit5
Pulsout 1, 1
pin0 = bit4
Pulsout 1, 1
pin0 = bit3
Pulsout 1, 1
pin0 = bit2
Pulsout 1, 1
pin0 = bit1
Pulsout 1, 1
pin0 = bit0
Pulsout 1, 1
```

```
Low 1
Return
```

The schematic shows that the parallel input lines to the 74LS165 are connected to V_{cc} through 10,000-Ω resistors. This puts a binary 1 on each input line. The switches used in this project are eight-position DIP switches. Each switch connects the bottom of a resistor to ground. When a switch is closed, it brings that particular pin to ground, or binary 0. By opening and closing the switches, we can write a binary number on the parallel input. This information is automatically retrieved from the 74LS165 serially by the PIC microcontroller.

The PIC microcontroller takes the number retrieved from the 74LS165 and displays it on the 74LS164. While this project may appear trivial, it is not. Using this information, you can set up serial communication routines with other chips and systems. In upcoming chapters, we will use a serial routine to communicate to a serial analog-to-digital (A/D) converter and use the Basic Serout command to generate LCD displays.

Parts List

Same as Chap. 1 (and Chap. 8 for programming challenge).

Additional components

74LS164	Serial-to-parallel IC
74LS165	Parallel-to-serial IC
(8)	10-kΩ $^1/_4$-W resistors
(1)	8-position DIP switch

Available from: Images Company, James Electronics, JDR MicroDevices, and RadioShack (see Suppliers Index).

LCD Alphanumeric Display

One thing PIC microcontrollers lack is some type of video display. With a display, the program could tell us what's happening inside the chip as it is running. The PIC could also output messages to the user and display the numeric value of a variable or register. A display would enhance the versatility of the microcontroller when given the ability to communicate and output messages to the user. The solution, however, is not a video display, but an alphanumeric LCD display. The LCD display we are using has two lines, 40 characters per line. The first 16 characters of each line are visible (more about this later). The balance of the characters on each line are off-screen.

The particular LCD module we are using receives standard serial data (RS-232) at either 2400 or 9600 baud. Finally we can use the Basic Serout commands. Asynchronous communication is time-dependent, meaning that it requires strict time control and framing of each bit transmitted. The reason is that there is no clock line telling the microcontroller when the information on the line is valid. Thus, time (starting at the start bit) becomes the sync factor.

In our previous serial examples, we have always had a clock line. Serial communication with a clock line is called *synchronous* communication. The time between transmitting or receiving bits can vary widely, from microseconds to days. The bit becomes valid only when the clock line clocks in the bit.

To communicate asynchronously (not in sync, or without a clock) requires the use of a start bit and a stop bit in addition to the strict time frame. As the name implies, the start bit informs the receiver that a byte of information is about to be transmitted. The start bit is followed by the bit information (usually 8 bits but sometimes 7 bits), which is followed by the stop bit.

Figure 9.1 illustrates a typical serial data communication. While the line is idle, it is in a Mark or Marking condition. The Mark is a binary 1, which may be a positive voltage or current. Binary 0 is sometimes referred to as a Space; it may be a zero-voltage or zero-current condition.

To initiate communication, the transmitter sends out a start bit (brings the line low). Next, the 8 data bits are sent. Notice that in this serial communica-

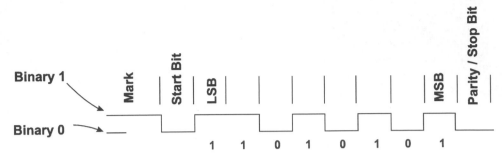

Figure 9.1 Standard serial output with start and stop bits.

tion, the LSB (least significant bit) is sent first and the MSB (most significant bit) is sent last. This is opposite to our previous synchronous serial communication examples.

A standard 8-bit data package plus 1 stop bit and 1 start bit equals a total of 10 bits. At 2400 baud (bits per second), 240 bytes are transmitted each second. At 9600 baud, a maximum of 960 bytes can be transmitted per second.

The frequency (baud rate) of asynchronous communication must be strictly adhered to. Since there isn't a clock line, the next bit in the sequence must be on the line for a precise increment of time that is determined by the baud rate. For instance, at 9600 baud, each bit is on the line for 104 μs (microseconds).

In order for things to work correctly, the transmitter and receiver frequency cannot vary from the ideal frequency by more than 5 percent. If their respective frequencies vary by more than that, during the course of 10 bits being transmitted and received, they can (but will not always) fall out of sync by more than a bit (104 μs). This sync error can corrupt the entire byte received.

Many people looking at a variance of 5 percent don't see how this could cause a problem. Let's do the math real quick and see how it happens. Let's assume that the transmitter is 5 percent faster than the ideal frequency and the receiver is 5 percent slower than the ideal frequency. For our example, the ideal frequency is 2400 baud, or 416.6 μs per bit. The transmitter is transmitting at 2520 baud (2400 plus 5 percent), or 396.8 μs per bit. The receiver is receiving at 2280 baud (2400 minus 5 percent), or 438.5 μs per bit. The difference is 41.7 μs per bit. Multiply this difference by 10 bits, and the timing is out by 417 μs. This is just a touch longer than the standard bit length of 416.6 μs at 2400 baud. So it becomes clear that if the frequency varies by more than 5 percent, the serial communication can fall out of sync, and be corrupted, by the time 10 bits have been transmitted and received.

Error Detection Algorithms

Full-featured communication packages may contain algorithms that will help prevent data corruption if the asynchronous time frame varies. Error detection algorithms have not yet become part of the PICBasic RS-232 communication routines.

Parity

The stop bit is used to check each byte transmitted, using a process known as parity. Parity may be odd, even, or none. The serial transmission consists of a sequence of binary 1s and 0s. If we choose even parity, the receiver will count how many binary 1s are transmitted. If the number of 1s transmitted is an even number, the stop bit will be made a binary 0, keeping the number of binary 1s even. On the other hand, if an odd number of binary 1s is transmitted, the stop bit will be made a binary 1 to make the number of 1s even.

If parity is set to even and an odd number of binary 1s is received, this is known as a *parity error* and the whole byte of information is thrown out. Parity errors may be caused by power surges, bad communication lines, or poor interface connections. The problems become more pronounced at faster baud rates.

Serial Formats

The PICBasic compiler has a few standard formats and speeds available. The available baud rates are 300, 1200, 2400, and 9600. Data are sent as 8 data bits, no parity, and 1 stop bit. The mode can be inverted. See the Serin and Serout commands in Chap. 5.

Crystal choice

When I first started using the Serin and Serout commands, they would not work properly. After much hair pulling, I discovered that I had used a 3.57 MHz crystal instead of a 4.0-MHz crystal on the PIC 16F84. As soon as I changed the crystal to a 4.0-MHz, the Serin and Serout commands worked perfectly. Later I tried a 4.0-MHz ceramic resonator for the oscillator, and this also worked properly.

Three-wire connection

The LCD display requires just three wires to function, +5 V, GND, and a serial line. The baud rate of the display may be set to either 9600 or 2400 baud. The serial format is 8 data bits, 1 stop bit, and no parity.

On the back of the LCD display, there is a five-pin header (see Fig. 9.2). The five-pin header has two extra pins for +5 V and GND. The pins are arranged in a palindrome layout, so a five-pin header may be connected either way and still be oriented correctly. Instead of using a five-pin header, I opted for a three-pin header socket connected to one side of the five-pin header.

Our first program prints out the message "Hello World." The cursor (printing position) automatically moves from left to right. The schematic is shown in Fig. 9.3.

```
' LCD Test
Pause 1000
Serout 1, N2400, (254, 1)
Pause 1
Serout 1, N2400, ("Hello World!")
End
```

Front View

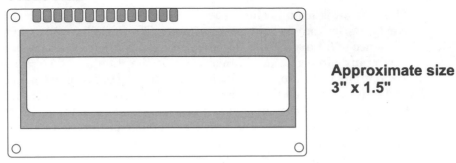

**Approximate size
3" x 1.5"**

Back View

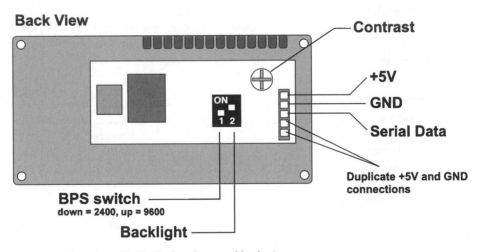

Figure 9.2 Drawing of LCD display, front and back views.

I kept this program small to show how easy it is to get a message out of the PIC microcontroller. Notice that line 2 of the program [Serout 1,N2400, (254,1)] is a command. The LCD screen has 13 commands. All commands must be prefixed with the decimal number 254. The display will treat any number following the 254 prefix as an instruction. The commands are listed in Table 9.1.

Positioning the Cursor

The cursor may be positioned anywhere on the LCD screen by using the following command: 254, position number. The position number can be determined by looking at Fig. 9.4. If we wanted to move the cursor to position 10 of the second line, we would use the command Serout 1, N2400, (254,201)

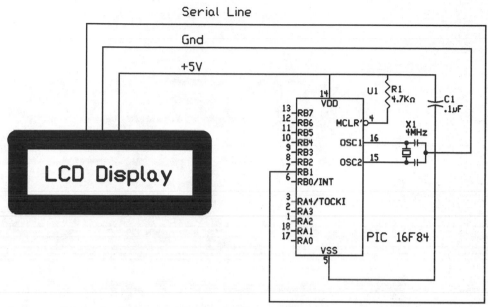

Figure 9.3 Schematic of LCD serial display to PIC 16F84 microcontroller.

TABLE 9.1 Instruction Codes for LCD Display

Code	Instruction
1	Clear screen
2	Send cursor to top left position (home)
8	Blank without clearing
12	Make cursor invisible/restore display if blanked
13	Turn on visible blinking cursor
14	Turn on visible underline cursor
16	Mover cursor one character left
20	Move cursor one character right
24	Scroll display one character left (all lines)
28	Scroll display one character right (all lines)

Off-Screen Memory

Each line of the LCD display holds 40 characters. Only the first 16 characters are displayed on the LCD screen. You can use the scroll commands to view the hidden text.

This second program illustrates moving the cursor to the second line (see Fig. 9.5).

LCD Display Screen

LCD Cursor Positions

Character Position	1	2	3	4	5	6	7	8	9	10	11	12	13	14	15	16
Line 1	128	129	130	131	132	133	134	135	136	137	138	139	140	141	142	143
Line 2	192	193	194	195	196	197	198	199	200	201	202	203	204	205	206	207

Figure 9.4 LCD display screen and cursor positions.

Figure 9.5 Picture of LCD display message.

```
' LCD test
Pause 1000
Serout 1, N2400, (254, 1)
Pause 2
Serout 1, N2400, ("Wherever you go.")
Serout 1, N2400, (254,192)
Pause 2
Serout 1, N2400, ("There you are.")
End
```

As we move forward, the LCD display will be invaluable for allowing us to peek inside the chip registers.

Parts List

Same components as in Chap. 1.

Additional components

LCD-01   Serial LCD Module Backlight $ 70.00
                Available from: Images Company, James Electronics, JDR MicroDevices, and
                RadioShack (see Suppliers Index).

Sensors: Resistive, Neural, and Fuzzy Logic

Reading Resistive Sensors

The Pot command is powerful in scope and capabilities. It allows users to easily and accurately read resistive components and sensors. The command can read resistive values up to approximately 50,000 Ω (50 kΩ) in a single program line. This command was first reviewed in Chap. 5.

```
Pot Pin, Scale, Var
```

This command reads a potentiometer or other resistive component on the *Pin* specified (see Fig. 10.1). The programmer may choose any of the port B pins, 0 to 7, to use with this command.

Resistance is measured by timing the discharge of a capacitor through the resistor, usually 5 to 50 kΩ. *Scale* is used to adjust varying *R/C* constants. For large *R/C* constants, set *Scale* to 1. For small *R/C* constants, set *Scale* to its maximum value of 255. Ideally if *Scale* is set correctly, the variable *Var* will be set to zero at minimum resistance and to 255 at maximum resistance.

R/C Values

Figure 10.2 graphs the decimal values generated by resistance for four common capacitor values. This chart should be used as a guide to determine the capacitance one could use for the resistance range one needs to read. For instance, using a 0.1-μF capacitor, the decimal values from 50 to 250 are equal to resistance values of 700 to 3500 Ω. For a 0.022-μF capacitor, the same decimal values equal a resistance range of 3500 Ω to 21 kΩ. Once a range is chosen, the scale factor in the command line may be used to fine-tune the response.

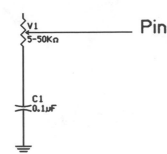

Figure 10.1 Resistive sensor (potentiometer) and capacitor connected to PIC pin.

Scale

Scale is determined experimentally. Set the device or transducer to measure at maximum resistance and read it with *Scale* set to 255. Under these conditions, the numeric value of *Var* produced will be an approximate "ideal" value for *Scale*.

Ideally, with a capacitor of the proper value and the proper scale, minimum resistance will output a numeric value close to zero and maximum resistance will output a numeric output close to 255.

Pin Exceptions

I/O pins that are listed as just TTL may be used with the Pot command. Pins listed as Schmitt triggers, or ST, do not appear to work with the Pot command. With the PICBasic compiler and the 16F84A, we are restricted to using the Pot command on port B pins only. It just so happens that three of the port B pins (RB0, RB6, and RB7) are listed as combination TTL/ST. Pins listed as TTL/ST on the 16F84A work with the Pot command.

The data sheet states that RB6 and RB7 are Schmitt trigger inputs when used in serial programming mode. RB0 is a Schmitt trigger input when configured as an external interrupt.

To ensure that the Pot command works with other PICMicros, look at the particular microcontroller's data sheet for any potential line problems.

Resistive Sensors

There are many resistive-type transducers that may be read using the Pot command. The important thing to remember is that the Pot command is not an analog-to-digital (A/D) converter. Converters measure analog voltages, not resistance.

This may at first be confusing, because converters can read a voltage drop across a resistor, and the drawing or schematic of reading a voltage drop may be similar in appearance to the Pot diagram; however, the diagrams are not the same. To determine the difference, the key point to look for is the absence of a voltage source on top of the resistive component being measured with the Pot command. A/D converters, on the other hand, will have a voltage or current source connected to the top of the resistor or sensor.

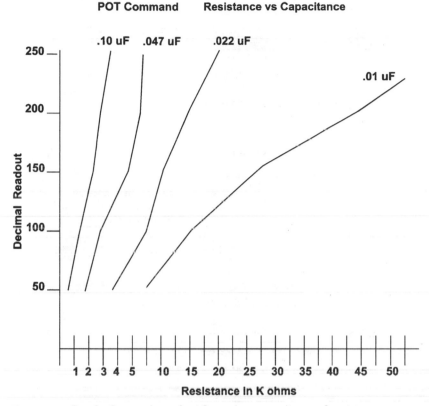

Figure 10.2 Graph of numeric readout for various capacitors and resistances.

Test Program

Okay, that's enough explanation; let's work with the command a little. The first resistive-type sensor we will look at is a flex sensor (see Fig. 10.3).

Flex sensors have numerous applications. For instance, they may be used as robotic whiskers for bump and wall sensors. They have been used to create virtual reality data gloves, physical measurements, and physics applications.

The program uses the LCD display from Chap. 9 to provide a visual readout. The numeric readout, *with the sensor at its maximum resistance*, provides the proper scale factor to use in the command in order to achieve the greatest range with this particular sensor. For my test, I plugged the flex sensor into the prototyping breadboard (see Fig. 10.4). The schematic for the project is shown in Fig. 10.5. Record the numeric readout when the sensor is at its maximum resistance, and use that for a scale factor for best range and accuracy.

Program 10.1

```
'Find scale factor and/or read the resistive sensor
start:
```

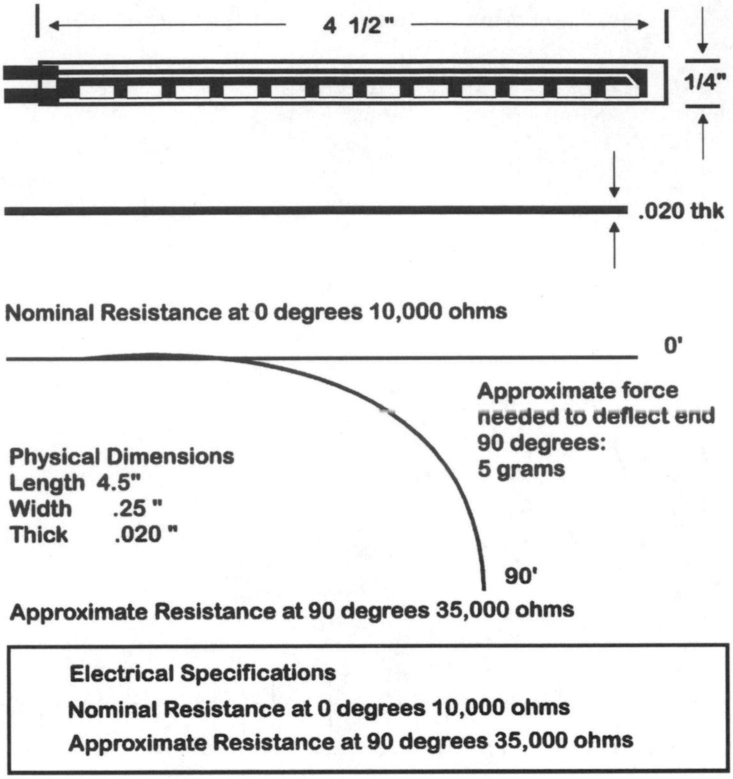

Nominal Resistance at 0 degrees 10,000 ohms

Physical Dimensions
Length 4.5"
Width   .25 "
Thick   .020 "

Approximate force
needed to deflect end
90 degrees:
5 grams

Approximate Resistance at 90 degrees 35,000 ohms

Electrical Specifications
Nominal Resistance at 0 degrees 10,000 ohms
Approximate Resistance at 90 degrees 35,000 ohms

Figure 10.3 Specification sheet on flex sensor.

```
Pot 1,255,B0               'Read resistance on pin 1 to
                           'determine scale
Serout 0,N2400,(254,1)     'Clear LCD screen
Serout 0,N2400, (#B0)      'Send Pot values out on pin 0 serially
Pause 500                  'Wait 1/2 s
Goto start                 'Do it again
```

If the scale factor displayed by Program 10.1 is 255 (or close to 255), the program is already reading the sensor at the best scale (with that particular capacitor).

We read the LCD display to determine that the program and the sensor are both working properly. The microcontroller, of course, does not require an LCD display in order to read the sensor. It can read the numeric value held in the variable and "interpret" the results.

Fuzzy Logic and Neural Sensors

We are presented with a few interesting possibilities regarding the interpretation of sensor readings. Here we can have the microcontroller mimic the function of a neural and/or fuzzy logic device.

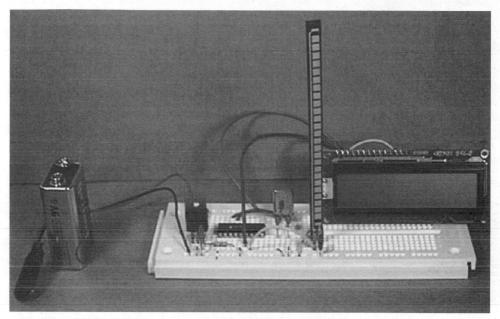

Figure 10.4 Photograph of flex sensor connected to PIC with LCD display.

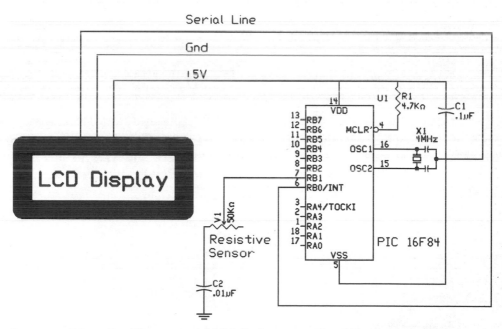

Figure 10.5 Schematic of flex sensor and LCD display connected to PIC microcontroller.

Fuzzy logic

In 1965, Lotfi Zadah, a professor at the University of California–Berkeley, first published a paper on fuzzy logic. Since its inception, fuzzy logic has been both hyped and criticized.

In essence, fuzzy logic attempts to mimic the way people apply logic in grouping and feature determination. A few examples should clear this "fuzzy" definition. For instance, how is a warm sunny day determined to be not warm but hot instead, and by whom? The threshold of when someone considers a warm day hot depends on the person's personal heat threshold and the influence of his or her environment (see Fig. 10.6).

There is no universal thermometer that states that at 81.9°F it is warm and at 82°F it is hot. Extending this example further, a person living in Alaska has a different set of temperature values for hot days from a person living in New York, and both these values will be different from those of someone living in Florida. And let's not forget seasonal variations. A hot day has a different temperature scale in winter from that in summer. So what all this boils down to is that the opinions of many people concerning the classification of a day as hot are grouped together.

Whether any particular temperature is a member of that group is determined by how closely that temperature matches the median value.

The same idea can be applied to many other things, such as navigation, speed, or height. Let's use height for one more example. If we graph the height of 1000 people, our graph will resemble the first graph shown in Fig. 10.7. We can use this graph of heights to classify shortness, average height, and tallness. If we applied a hard rule that stated that everyone under 5'7" is short and everyone taller than 6'0" is tall, our graph would resemble the second graph. What this does is classify someone who is 5'11.5" inches tall as average, when in actuality the person's height is closer to that of the tall (6'0" and over) group.

Instead of hard rules, people typically use soft and imprecise logic, or fuzzy logic. Fuzzy logic uses groups and quantifies the membership in each group. Groups overlap, as seen in the fourth graph. So the person who is 5'11.5" tall is almost out of the medium group (small membership) and well into the tall group (large membership).

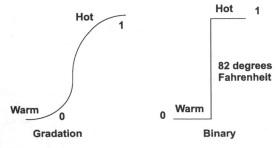

Figure 10.6 Two graphs of temperature change, gradual and steep.

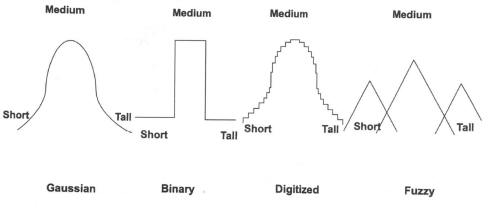

Figure 10.7   Four graphs of height: gaussian, binary, digitized, and fuzzy.

Fuzzy logic provides an alternative to the digitized graph (the third graph). A high-resolution digitized graph is also accurate in classifying height. Why would one choose the fuzzy logic method over a digitized model function? Simplified mathematics and learning functions.

To implement fuzzy logic in a PIC microcontroller, one assigns a numeric range to a group. This is what we will do in our next project.

Fuzzy Logic Light Tracker

The next project we will build is a fuzzy logic light tracker. The tracker follows a light source using fuzzy logic.

The sensor needed for the tracker is a cadmium sulfide (CdS) photocell. A photocell is a light-sensitive resistor (see Fig. 10.8). Its resistance varies in proportion to the intensity of the light falling on its surface. In complete darkness, the cell produces its greatest resistance.

There are many types of CdS cells on the market. One chooses a particular cell based on its dark resistance and light saturation resistance. The term *light saturation* refers to the state in which increasing the light intensity to the CdS cell will not decrease its resistance any further. It is saturated. The CdS cell I used has approximately 100 kΩ resistance in complete darkness and 500 Ω resistance when totally saturated with light. Under ambient light, resistance varies between 2.5 and 10 kΩ.

To ascertain the proper scale factor, we first decide what capacitor we should use for the best overall range. We then connect the sensor to the PIC microcontroller and run the scale program. The scale factor is used in the program.

The project requires two CdS cells. Test each cell separately. There may be a within-group variance that may change the scale factor used for a particular cell. In this project, I used a 0.022-μF capacitor, with the scale parameter set at 255 for both cells in the Pot command.

The schematic is shown in Fig. 10.9. The CdS cells are connected to port B pins 2 and 3 (physical pin numbers 8 and 9). The photocells are mounted on a

Cadmium Sulfide

Electronic Symbols

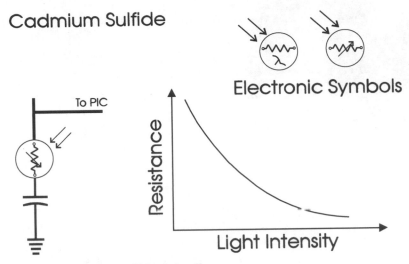

Figure 10.8   Cadmium sulfide photocell.

small piece of wood or plastic (see Fig. 10.10). For each CdS cell, two small holes are drilled for the wire leads to pass through. Longer wires are soldered to these wires and connected to the PIC microcontroller.

One $^3/_{32}$- to $^1/_8$-in hole is drilled for the gearbox motor's shaft. The sensor array is glued to the gearbox motor shaft (see Fig. 10.11).

The operation of the tracker is shown in Fig. 10.12. When both sensors are equally illuminated, their respective resistances are approximately the same. As long as each sensor is within ±10 points of the other, the PIC program sees them as equal and doesn't initiate movement. This provides a group range of 20 points. This group range is the fuzzy part in fuzzy logic.

When either sensor falls in shadow, its resistance increases beyond our range, and the PIC microcontroller activates the motor to bring both sensors under even illumination.

DC motor control

The light tracker uses a gearbox motor to rotate the sensor array toward the light source (see Fig. 10.13). The gearbox motor shown has a 4000:1 ratio. The shaft spins at approximately 1 rpm. You need a suitably slow motor (gearbox) to turn the sensor array.

The sensor array is attached (glued) to the shaft of the gearbox motor. The gearbox motor can rotate the sensor array clockwise (CW) or counterclockwise (CCW), depending upon the direction of the current flowing through the motor.

To rotate the shaft (and sensor array) CW and CCW, we need a way to reverse the current going to the motor. We will use what is known as an H-bridge. An H-bridge uses four transistors (see Fig. 10.14). Consider each transistor as a simple on and off switch, as shown in the top portion of the drawing. It's called an H-bridge because the transistors (switches) are arranged in an H pattern.

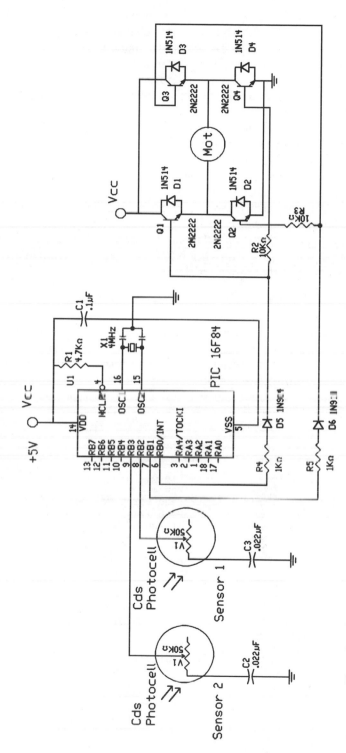

Figure 10.9 Fuzzy logic light tracker circuit.

When switches SW1 and SW4 are closed, the motor rotates in one direction. When switches SW2 and SW3 are closed, the motor rotates in the opposite direction. When all the switches are opened, the motor is stopped.

The PIC microcontroller controls the H-bridge, which is made of four TIP120 Darlington NPN transistors, four 1N514 diodes, and two 10-kΩ ¼-W resistors. Pin 0 is connected to transistors Q1 and Q4, and pin 1 is connected to transistors Q3 and Q4. Using either pin 0 or pin 1, the proper transistors are turned on and off to achieve CW or CCW rotation. The microcontroller can stop, rotate CW, or rotate CCW, depending upon the reading from the sensor array.

Make sure that the 10-kΩ resistors are placed properly or the H-bridge will not function.

The TIP120 Darlington transistors are drawn in the schematic as standard NPN transistors. Many H-bridge circuit designs use PNP transistors on the high side of the H-bridge. The on resistance of PNP transistors is higher than NPN transistors. So, in using NPN transistors exclusively in our H-bridge, we achieve a slightly higher efficiency.

Diodes

Because the PIC is sensitive to electrical spikes (they may cause a reset or lockup), we place diodes across the collector-emitter junction of each transistor (Q1 to Q4). These diodes snub any electrical spikes caused by switching the motor's windings on and off.

Program 10.2

```
'Fuzzy logic light tracker
start:
Low 0                       'Pin 0 low
Low 1                       'Pin 1 low
Pot 2,255,b0               'Read first CdS sensor
Pot 3,255,b1               'Read second CdS sensor
If b0 = b1 Then start      'If equal, do nothing
If b0 > b1 Then greater    'If greater, check how much greater
If b0 < b1 Then lesser     'If lesser, check how much lesser
greater:                    'Greater routine
b2 = b0 - b1               'Find the difference
If b2 > 10 Then cw         'Is it within range? If not, go to cw
Goto start                  'If it is in range, do it again
lesser:                     'Lesser routine
b2 = b1 - b0               'Find the difference
If b2 > 10 Then ccw        'Is it within range? If not go to ccw
Goto start                  'Do again
cw:                         'Turn the sensor array clockwise
High 0                      'Turn on H-bridge
Pause 100                   'Let it turn for a moment
Goto start                  'Check again
ccw:                        'Turn the sensor array counterclockwise
High 1                      'Turn on H-bridge
Pause 100                   'Let it turn a moment
Goto start                  'Check again
```

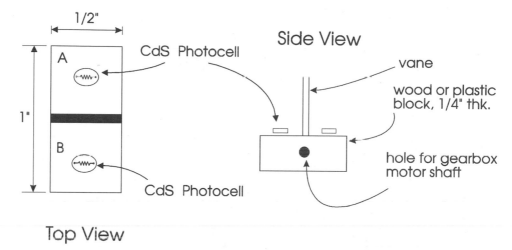

Figure 10.10   Sensor array.

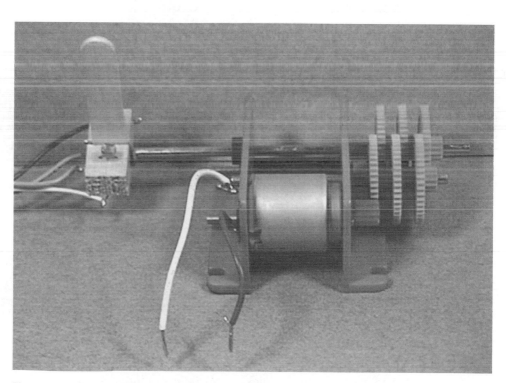

Figure 10.11   Sensor array connected to shaft of gearbox motor.

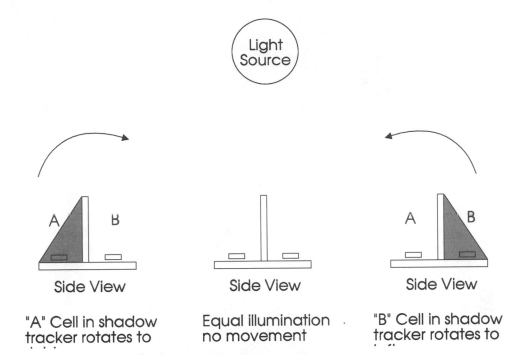

Figure 10.12 Functional behavior of sensor array.

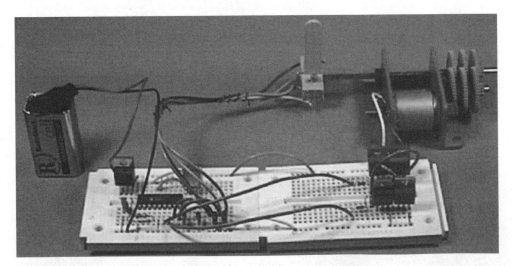

Figure 10.13   Photograph of fuzzy light tracking circuit.

Operation

When run, the light tracker will follow a light source. If both CdS cells are approximately evenly illuminated, the tracker does nothing. To test this, cover one CdS sensor with your finger. This should activate the gearbox motor, and the shaft should begin to rotate.

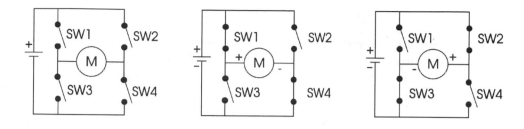

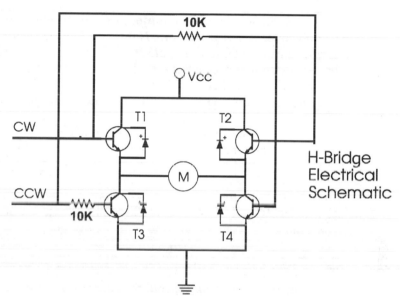

Figure 10.14 H-bridge function and electrical schematic.

If the shaft rotates in the direction opposite the light source, reverse either the sensor input pins or the output pins to the H-bridge, but not both.

Fuzzy Output

The output of our fuzzy light tracker is binary. The motor is either on or off, rotating clockwise or counterclockwise. In many cases you would want the output to be fuzzy also. For instance, let's say you're making a fuzzy controller for elevators. You would want the elevator to start and stop gradually (fuzzy) not abruptly as in binary (on-off).

Could we change the output of our light tracker and make it fuzzy? Yes. Instead of simply switching the motor on, we could feed a PWM (pulse-width-modulation) signal that can vary the motor's speed.

Ideally, the motor's speed would be in proportion to the difference (in resistance) of the two CdS cells. A large difference would produce a faster speed than a small difference. The motor speed would change dynamically (in real time) as the tracker brings both CdS cells to equal illumination.

This output program may be illustrated using fuzzy logic graphics, groups, and membership sets.

In this particular application, creating a fuzzy output for this demonstration light tracker unit is overkill. If you want to experiment, begin by using the Pulsout and PWM commands to vary the dc motor speed.

Neural sensors (logic)

With a small amount of programming, we can change our fuzzy logic sensors (CdS photocells) to neural sensors. Neural networks are an expansive topic; we are limiting ourselves to one small example. For those who want to pursue further study into neural networks, I recommend a book I've written entitled *Understanding Neural Networks* (ISBN #0-7906-1115-5).

To create neural sensors, we will take the numeric resistive reading from each sensor, multiply it by a weight factor, and then sum the results. The results are then compared to a tri-level threshold value (see Fig. 10.15).

Thus, our small program and sensors are performing all the functions expected in a neural network. We may even be pioneering a neural first, by applying a multivalue threshold scheme. Are multivalue thresholds natural or mimicked in nature (biological systems)? The answer is yes. For instance, an itch is a extremely low level of pain. The sensation of burning is actually the combination of sensing ice cold with warm (ooh).

Multivalue threshold

Typically in neural networks, individual neurons have a singular threshold (positive or negative) that, once exceeded, activates the output of the neuron. In our example, the output is compared to multiple values, with the output going to the best fit.

Instead of thinking of the output as numeric values, think of each numeric range as a shape instead; a circle, square, and triangle will suffice. When the neuron is summed, it outputs a shape block (instead of a number). The receptor neurons (LEDs) have a shaped receiver unit that can fit in a shape block. When a shape block matches the receiver unit, the neuron becomes active (LED turns on).

In our case, each output neuron relates to a particular behavior: sleeping, hunting, and feeding—behaviors essential for survival in a photovore-style robot. Each output shape represents the current light level.

Low light level: The photovore stops hunting and searching for food (light). It enters a sleep or hibernation mode.

Medium light level: The photovore hunts and searches for the brightest light areas.

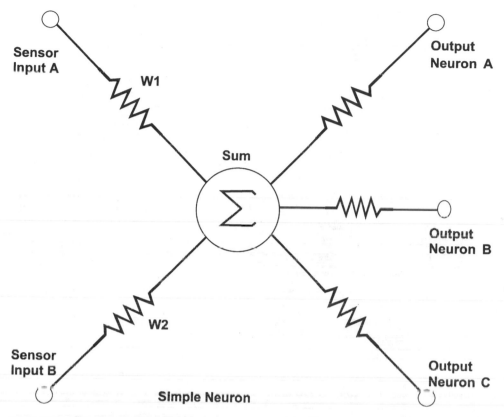

Figure 10.15 Simple neural sensor.

High light level: The photovore stops and feeds via solar cells to recharge its batteries.

Instead of building a photovore robot, we will use an LED to distinguish among the behavior states (see schematic in Fig. 10.16). You can label the LEDs sleeping, hunting, and feeding. Which LED will become active will depend upon the light level received by the CdS cells. The finished project is shown in Fig. 10.17.

Program 10.3

```
'Neural demo
'Set up
Low 0                    'LED 0 off: "Sleep"
Low 1                    'LED 1 off: "Hunt"
Low 2                    'LED 2 off: "Feed"
Start:
Pot 3,255,b0             'Read first sensor
Pot 4,255,b1             'Read second sensor
w2 = b0 * 3             'Apply weight
```

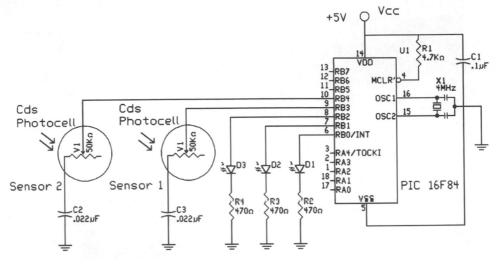

Figure 10.16   Neural microcontroller circuit.

Figure 10.17   Photograph of neural microcontroller circuit.

```
w3 = b1 * 2              'Apply weight
w4 = w2 + w3             'Sum results
'Apply thresholds
If w4 < 40 Then feed     'Lots of light; feed
If w4 <= 300 Then hunt   'Medium light; hunt
If w4 > 300 Then snooze  'Little light; sleep
'Actions
```

```
feed:                    `Feeding
Low 0
Low 1
High 2
Goto start
hunt:                    `Hunting
Low 0
High 1
Low 2
Goto start
snooze:                  `Sleeping. DON'T USE KEYWORD SLEEP
High 0
Low 1
Low 2
Goto start
```

Parts List

Components outlined in Chap. 1.

Additional components

- (2) CdS photocells
- (1) Flex sensor
- (2) 0.022-μF capacitors
- (1) 0.01-μF capacitor
- (4) TIP120 NPN Darlington transistors
- (2) 10-kΩ resistors
- (6) 1N514 diodes
- (2) 1-kΩ resistors
- (1) Gearbox motor

Available from: Images Company, James Electronics, JDR MicroDevices, and RadioShack (see Suppliers Index).

Chapter 1

DC Motor Control

In this chapter we will look at a few methods of controlling a dc hobby motor.

A single pin of the 16F84 PIC microcontroller is limited to a maximum output current of 25 mA. In most cases, this is too feeble a current to power a dc motor directly. Instead, we use the output of a PIC pin to turn on and off a transistor that can easily control the current needed to run hobby motors. The two methods we use incorporate transistors to switch current on and off.

The Transistor

The transistor of choice used in most of these examples is a TIP120 NPN transistor. The TIP120 is a Darlington transistor, medium power, 5 A maximum current, and designed for general-purpose amplification and low-speed switching. The PNP version of this transistor is the TIP125.

First Method

This is a simple on-off motor switch (see Fig. 11.1). When the PIC pin is brought high, the transistor goes into conduction, thereby turning on the dc motor. The diode across the collector-emitter junction of the transistor protects the transistor from any inductive voltage surge caused by switching the motor off. For added PIC protection, insert a signal diode and current-limiting resistor on the output pin.

```
'Program dc motor
Pause 1000          'Wait 1 s
High 0              'Turn on dc motor
Pause 1000          'Wait 1 s
Low 0               'Turn off dc motor
End
```

In the circuit, notice the 1500-μF capacitor. A large capacitor is needed to smooth the voltage dips caused by the dc motor's turning on and off. Without a large capacitor, the sudden dip in voltage may inadvertently reset the PIC microcontroller. A picture of this circuit is shown in Fig. 11.2.

Bidirectional Method

An H-bridge allows bidirectional control of a dc motor. To achieve this, it uses four transistors (see Fig. 11.3). Consider each transistor as a simple on-off switch, as shown in the top portion of the drawing. This circuit is called an H-bridge because the transistors (switches) are arranged in an H pattern.

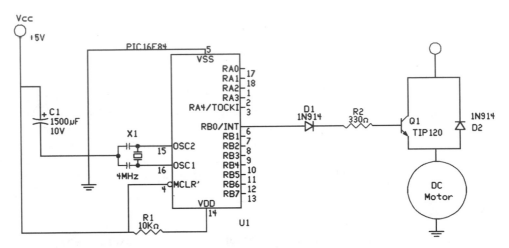

Figure 11.1   On-off motor switch using TIP120 transistor.

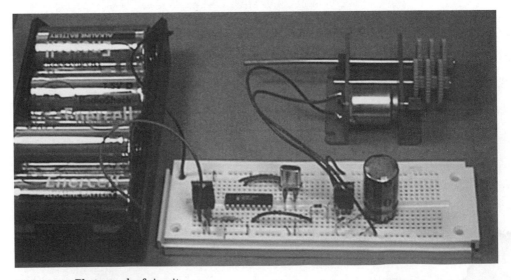

Figure 11.2   Photograph of circuit.

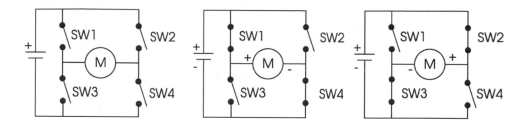

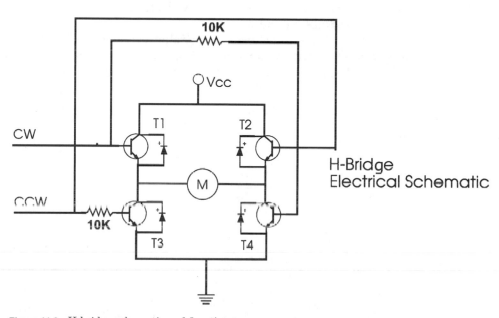

H-Bridge
Electrical Schematic

Figure 11.3 H-bridge schematic and function.

When switches SW1 and SW4 are closed, the motor rotates in one direction. When switches SW2 and SW3 are closed, the motor rotates in the opposite direction. When all the switches are open, the motor is stopped. Replace the switches with transistors and you have an electronic H-bridge.

The PIC microcontroller controls an H-bridge made of four TIP120 Darlington NPN transistors, four 1N514 diodes, and two 10-kΩ ¼-W resistors (see Fig. 11.4). The TIP120 Darlington transistors are drawn in the schematic as standard NPN transistors. Pin 0 is connected to transistors Q1 and Q4. Pin 1 is connected to transistors Q3 and Q4. Using either pin 0 or pin 1, the proper transistors are turned on and off to achieve clockwise (CW) or counterclockwise (CCW) rotation. If, by accident or programming error, pins 0 and 1 are brought high simultaneously, this will create a short circuit.

If the H-bridge is used properly, the microcontroller can stop, rotate CW, or rotate CCW the DC motor.

Many H-bridge circuit designs use PNP transistors on the high side of the H-bridge. The on resistance of PNP transistors is higher than NPN transistors. So, in using NPN transistors exclusively in our H-bridge, we achieve a slightly higher efficiency.

Diodes

Because the PIC is sensitive to electrical spikes (they may cause a reset or lockup), we place diodes across the collector-emitter junction of each transistor (Q1 to Q4). These diodes snub any electrical spikes caused by switching the motor's windings on and off.

A picture of the PIC H-bridge controller is shown in Fig. 11.5. The following program rotates the motor CW for 1 s, pauses for 0.5 s, then rotates the motor CCW for 1 s, pauses for 0.5 s, and then repeats the sequence.

```
`H-bridge
Low 0
Low 1
start:
Pause 500          `Pause for 0.5 s
High 1          `Rotate motor in one direction
Pause 1000          `Wait 1 s
Low 1          `Stop motor
Pause 500          `Pause for 0.5 s
```

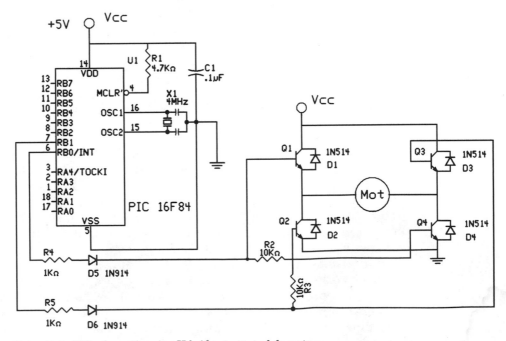

Figure 11.4 PIC schematic using H-bridge to control dc motor.

```
High 0          'Rotate in opposite direction
Pause 1000      'Wait 1 s
Low 0           'Stop motor
Goto start      'Do it again
```

Parts List

Same components as in Chap. 1.

Additional components

(4) TIP120 NPN Darlington transistors

(2) 10-kΩ resistors

(1) Dc motor

(4) 1N914 signal diodes

Available from: Images Company, James Electronics, JDR MicroDevices, and RadioShack (see Suppliers Index).

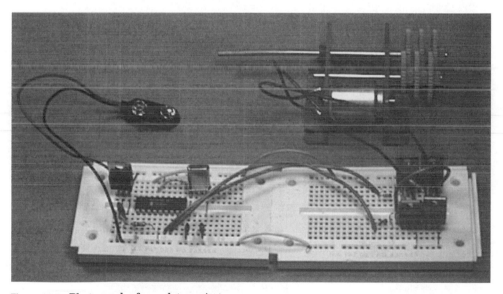

Figure 11.5 Photograph of complete project.

Stepper Motor Control

In the last chapter, we programmed the PIC microcontroller to control dc motors. Along with dc motors, stepper motors and servomotors are types of motors that are commonly used. In this chapter we will examine the use of stepper motors.

Stepper motors provide considerable advantages over dc motors. Under a PIC controller, stepper motors may be used for precise positioning in a wide range of applications, including robotics, automation, animatronics, and positioning control.

Stepper motors operate differently from dc motors. When power is applied to a dc motor, the rotor begins turning smoothly. Speed is measured in revolutions per minute (rpm) and is a function of voltage, current, and load on the motor. Precise positioning of the motor's rotor is usually not possible or desirable.

A stepper motor, on the other hand, runs on a sequence of electric pulses to the windings of the motor. Each pulse rotates the stepper motor's rotor by a precise increment. Each increment of the rotor movement is referred to as a step—hence the name *stepper motor*. The incremental steps of the rotor's rotation translate to a high degree of positioning control, either rotationally or linearly if the stepper motor is configured to produce linear motion. The incremental rotation is measured in degrees.

Stepper motors are manufactured with varying degrees of rotation per step. The specifications of any particular stepper motor will always state the degree of rotation per step. You can find stepper motors with degrees per step that vary from a fraction of a degree (0.12°) to many degrees (e.g., 22.5°).

To become familiar with stepper motors, we will build a simple stepper motor controller from a PIC 16F84 and examine the operating principles of stepper motors.

Stepper Motor Construction and Operation

Stepper motors are constructed using strong permanent magnets and electromagnets. The permanent magnets are located on the rotating shaft, called the *rotor*. The electromagnets or windings are located on the stationary portion of the motor, called the *stator*. Figure 12.1 illustrates a stepper motor stepping through one complete rotation. The stator, or stationary portion of the motor, surrounds the rotor.

In Fig. 12.1, position 1, we start with the rotor facing the upper electromagnet, which is turned on. To move the rotor in a clockwise (CW) rotation, the upper electromagnet is switched off and the electromagnet to the right is switched on. This causes the rotor to rotate 90° CW to align itself with the electromagnet, shown in position 2. Continuing in the same manner, the rotor is stepped through a full rotation until we end up in the same position as we started, shown in position 5.

Resolution

The amount of rotation per pulse is the *resolution* of the stepper motor. In the example illustrated in Fig. 12.1, the rotor turned 90° per pulse—not a very practical motor. A practical stepper motor has a greater resolution (smaller steps); for instance, it may rotate its shaft 1° per pulse (or step). Such a motor requires 360 pulses (or steps) to complete one revolution.

When a stepper motor is used for positioning in a linear motion table, each step of the motor translates to a precise increment of linear movement.

Assume that one revolution of the motor is equal to 1 in. of linear travel on the table. For a stepper motor that rotates 3.75° per step, the increment of linear movement is approximately 0.01 in. per step. A stepper motor that rotates 1.0° per step would give approximately 0.0027 in. per step. The increment of movement is inversely proportional to the number of degrees per step.

Half-stepping

It is possible to double the resolution of some stepper motors by a process known as half-stepping. The process is illustrated in Fig. 12.2. In position I, the motor starts with the upper electromagnet switched on, as before. In position II, the electromagnet to the right is switched on while power to the upper coil remains on. Since both coils are on, the rotor is equally attracted to both electromagnets and positions itself in between the two positions (a half-step). In position III, the upper electromagnet is switched off and the rotor completes one step. Although I am only showing one half-step, the motor can be half-stepped through the entire rotation.

Other types of stepper motors

There are four-wire stepper motors. These stepper motors are called bipolar and have two coils, with a pair of leads to each coil. Although the circuitry of this stepper motor is simpler than that of the motor we are using, this motor requires a more complex driving circuit. The circuit must be able to reverse the current flow in the coils after it steps.

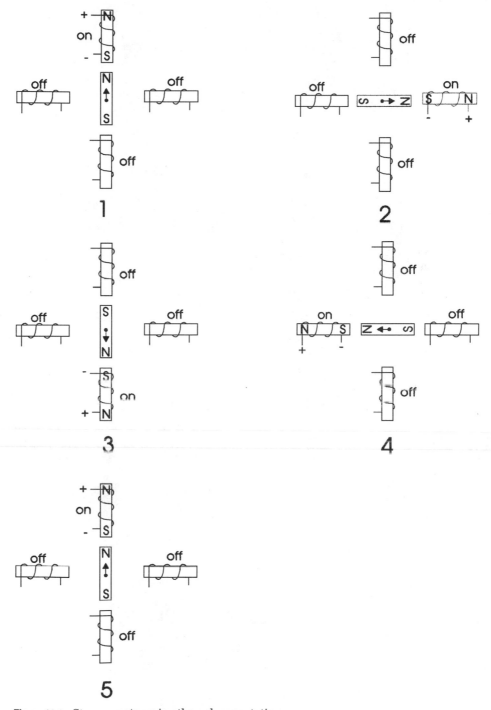

Figure 12.1 Stepper motor going through one rotation.

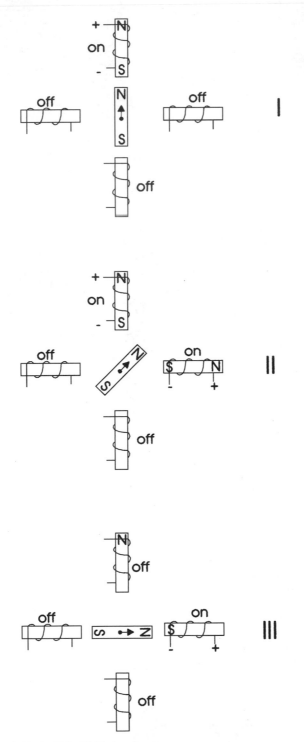

Figure 12.2 Half-stepping.

Real-World Motors

The stepper motor illustrated in Figs. 12.1 and 12.2 rotated 90° per step. Real-world stepper motors employ a series of mini-poles on the stator and rotor. The mini-poles reduce the number of degrees per step and improve the resolution of the stepper motor. Although the drawing in Fig. 12.3 appears more complex, the operation of the motor is identical to that of the motors shown in Figs. 12.1 and 12.2.

The rotor in Fig. 12.3 is turning in a CW rotation. In position I, the north pole of the permanent magnet on the rotor is aligned with the south pole of the electromagnet on the stator. Notice that there are multiple positions that are all lined up. In position II, the electromagnet is switched off and the coil to its immediate left is switched on. This causes the rotor to rotate CW by a precise amount. It continues in this same manner for each step. After eight steps, the sequence of electric pulses starts to repeat.

Half-stepping with the multipole arrangement is identical to the half-stepping described before.

First Stepper Circuit

Figure 12.4 is the schematic for our first test circuit. The output lines from the PIC 16F84 are buffered using a 4050 hex buffer chip. Each buffered signal line is connected to an NPN transistor. The TIP120 transistor is actually an NPN Darlington; in the schematic, it is shown as a standard NPN. The TIP120 transistors act like switches, turning on one stepper motor coil at a time.

Multipole Operation

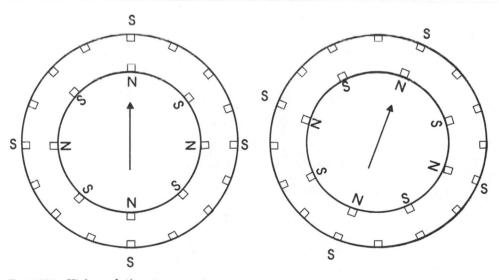

Figure 12.3 High-resolution stepper motor.

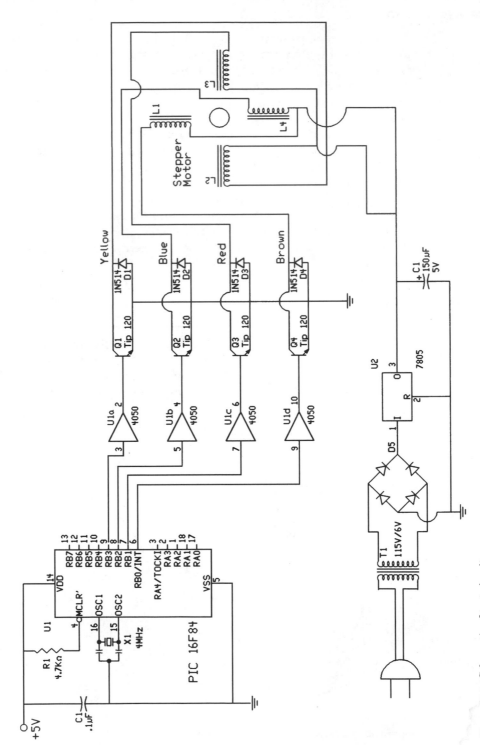

Figure 12.4 Schematic of test circuit.

The diode placed across each transistor protects the transistor from the inductive surge created when current is switched on and off in the stepper motor coils. The diode provides a safe return path for the reverse current. Without the diodes, the transistor will be more prone to failure and/or shorter life.

Stepper motors

Figure 12.5 is an electric equivalent circuit of the stepper motor we are using. The stepper motor has six wires coming out from the casing. We can see by following the lines that three leads go to each half of the coil windings, and that the coil windings are connected in pairs. This is how unipolar four-phase stepper motors are wired.

So, let's assume that you just picked this stepper motor and didn't know anything about it. The simplest way to analyze it is to check the electrical resistance between the leads. By making a table of the resistances measured between the leads, you'll quickly find which wires are connected to which coils.

Figure 12.6 shows how the resistance of the motor we are using looks. There is a 13-Ω resistance between the center-tap wire and each end lead, and 26 Ω between the two end leads. The resistance reading from wires originating from separate coils will be infinitely high (no connection). For instance, this would be the case for the resistance between the blue and brown leads.

Armed with this information, you can decipher just about any six-wire stepper motor you come across and wire it properly into a circuit. The stepper motor we are using rotates 1.8° per step.

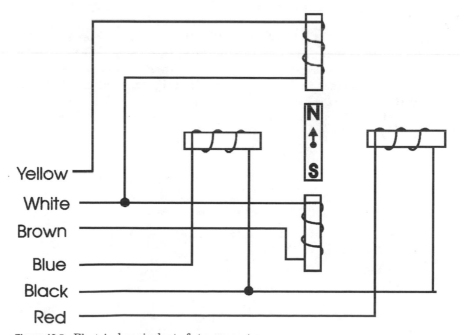

Figure 12.5 Electrical equivalent of stepper motor.

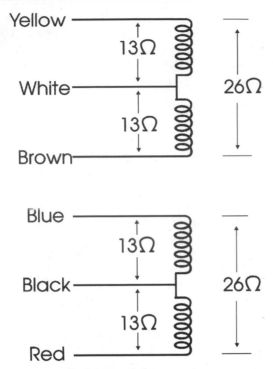

Figure 12.6   Resistance of stepper motor.

First test circuit and program

After you are finished constructing the test circuit, program the PIC with the following Basic program. The program has been kept small and simple to show how easy it is to get a stepper motor moving. Table 12.1 shows that each step in the sequence turns on one transistor. Use the table to follow the logic in the PICBasic program.

When you reach the end of the table, the sequence repeats, starting back at the top of the table.

```
'Stepper motor controller
Symbol TRISB = 134          'Initialize TRISB to 134
Symbol PortB = 6            'Initialize variable PortB to 6
Symbol ti = b6              'Initial ti delay
ti = 25                     'Set delay to 25 ms
Poke TRISB,0                'Set port B lines output
start:                      'Forward rotation sequence
Poke portB,1                'Step 1
Pause ti                    'Delay
Poke portB,2                'Step 2
Pause ti                    'Delay
Poke portB,4                'Step 3
Pause ti                    'Delay
Poke portB,8                'Step 4
Pause ti                    'Delay
Goto start                  'Do it again
```

TABLE 12.1 Full-Stepping

Transistors				Port B output (decimal)
Q1	Q2	Q3	Q4	
On	—	—	—	1
—	On	—	—	2
—	—	On	—	4
—	—	—	On	8

One rotation

Using whole steps, the stepper motor requires 200 pulses to complete a single rotation (360°/1.8° per step). Having the PIC microcontroller count pulses allows it to control and position the stepper motor's rotor.

Second Basic Program

This second PICBasic program is far more versatile. The user can modify programmed parameters (time delay) as the program is running, using one of the four switches connected to port A. Pressing SW1 lengthens the delay pause between steps in the sequence and consequently makes the stepper motor rotate more slowly. Pressing SW2 has the opposite effect. Pressing SW3 makes the program halt the stepper motor and stay in a holding loop for as long as SW3 is closed (or pressed). Rotation direction (CW or CCW) is controlled with the SW4 switch. Pressing the SW4 switch reverses the stepper motor direction. The direction stays in reverse for as long as SW4 is pressed (or closed).

```
'Stepper motor controller
Symbol TRISB = 134        'Initialize TRISB to 134
Symbol TRISA = 133        'Initialize TRISA to 133
Symbol portB = 6          'Initialize variable portB to 6
Symbol portA = 5          'Initialize variable portA to 5
Symbol ti = b6            'Initial ti delay
ti = 100                  'Set delay to 100 ms
Poke TRISB,0              'Set port B lines output
start:                    'Forward stepper motor rotation sequence
sequence
Poke portB,1              'Step 1
Pause ti                  'Delay
Poke portB,2              'Step 2
Pause ti                  'Delay
Poke portB,4              'Step 3
Pause ti                  'Delay
Poke portB,8              'Step 4
Pause ti                  'Delay
Goto check                'Jump to check switch status
start2:                   'Reverse motor rotation sequence
```

```
Poke portB,8          'Step 1
Pause ti              'Delay
Poke portB,4          'Step 2
Pause ti              'Delay
Poke portB,2          'Step 3
Pause ti              'Delay
Poke portB,1          'Step 4
Pause ti              'Delay
Goto check            'Jump to check switch status
check:                'Switch status
Peek portA, B0        'Peek the switches
If bit0 = 0 Then loop1    'If SW1 is closed, increase ti
If bit1 = 0 Then loop2    'If SW2 is closed, decrease ti
If bit2 = 0 Then hold3    'Stop motor
If bit3 = 0 Then start    'Go forward
Goto start2           'Go reverse
loop1:                'Increase delay
Poke portB,0          'Turn off transistors
ti = ti + 5           'Increase delay by 5 ms
Pause 50              'Delay
If ti > 250 Then hold1    'Limit delay to 250 ms
Peek portA,b0         'Check switch status
If bit0 = 0 Then loop1    'Still increasing delay?
Goto check            'If not, jump to main switch status check
loop2:                'Decrease delay
Poke portB,0          'Turn off transistors
ti = ti - 5           'Decrease delay by 5 ms
Pause 50              'Pause
If ti < 20 Then hold2     'Limit delay to 20 ms
Peek portA,b0         'Check switch status
If bit1 = 0 Then loop2    'Still decreasing delay?
Goto check            'If not, jump to main switch status check
hold1:                'Limit upper delay
ti = 245              'To 245 ms
Goto loop1            'Go back
hold2:                'Limit lower delay
ti = 25               'To 25 ms
goto loop2            'Go back
hold3:                'Stop stepper motor
Poke portB,0          'Turn off transistor
Peek portA, b0        'Check switches
If bit2 = 0 Then hold3    'Keep motor off?
Goto check            'If not, jump to main switch status check
```

The schematic for this program is shown in Fig. 12.7. In the photograph of the circuit (see Fig. 12.8), the four switches are difficult to make out. They are the four bare wire strips behind the PIC microcontroller. The top sides of the bare wire strips are connected to +5 V through 10-kΩ resistors. A wire from each switch is connected to the appropriate pin on port A. A single wire is connected to ground and is used to close any of the switches by touching the bare wire strip.

Half-Stepping

Half-stepping the motor effectively doubles the resolution. In this instance, it will require 400 pulses to complete one rotation. Table 12.2 shows the switch-

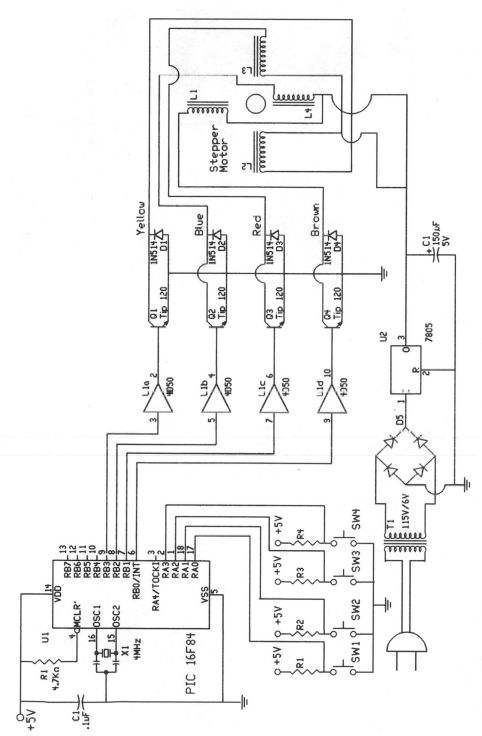

Figure 12.7 Schematic of stepper motor circuit.

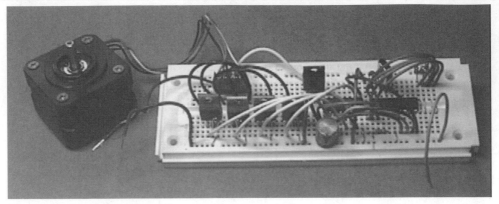

Figure 12.8 Photograph of circuit.

TABLE 12.2   Half-Stepping

Transistors				
Q1	Q2	Q3	Q4	Port B output (decimal)
On	—	—	—	1
On	On	—	—	3
—	On	—	—	2
—	On	On	—	6
—	—	On	—	4
—	—	On	On	12
—	—	—	On	8
On	—	—	On	9

ing logic needed in a program.

When you reach the end of the table, the sequence repeats, starting back at the top of the table.

The ti Delay Variable

The ti variable used in each Basic program controls a delay pause whose purpose is to slow down the output sequence to port B. Without the pause, the sequence might run too fast for the stepper motor to respond, causing the stepper motor to malfunction.

You may want to vary the ti variable in the program depending upon your PIC crystal speed. You can experiment with the ti variable until you find the best range for your particular PIC.

Troubleshooting

If the motor doesn't move at all, check the diodes. Make sure you have them in properly, facing in the direction shown in the schematic.

If the stepper motor moves slightly and/or quivers back and forth, there are a number of possible causes.

1. If you are using a battery power supply, the batteries may be too weak to power the motor properly. *Note*: Batteries wear out quickly because the current draw from stepper motors is usually high.

2. If you substituted another transistor for the TIP 120 NPN transistor, the substitute transistor may not be switching properly or the current load of the stepper motor may be too great. *Solution*: Use TIP 120 transistors.

3. You have the stepper motor improperly wired into the circuit. Check the coils using an ohmmeter and rewire if necessary.

4. The pulse frequency is too high. If the pulses to the stepper motor are going faster than the motor can react, the motor will malfunction. The solution to this problem is to reduce the pulse frequency. The pulse frequency is controlled by the ti variable in the program. Increasing the value of this variable will slow down the pulse frequency to the stepper motor.

UCN 5804 Dedicated Stepper Motor ICs

We have controlled the stepper motor directly from the PIC chip. There are dedicated integrated circuits that we can use to control stepper motors. If we incorporate stepper motor controller chips into the design, the PIC controller can control multiple stepper motors. These controller chips can do most of the grunt work of controlling a stepper motor. This simplifies our program and overall circuit while enhancing the hardware—a good combination.

One chip I use frequently is the UCN 5804 stepper motor controller. The pinout of the UCN 5804 is shown in Fig. 12.9. Features of the UCN 5804 are as follows:

- 1.25-A maximum output current (continuous)
- 35-V output sustaining voltage
- Full-step and half-step outputs
- Output enable and direction control
- Internal clamp diodes
- Power-on reset
- Internal thermal shutdown circuitry

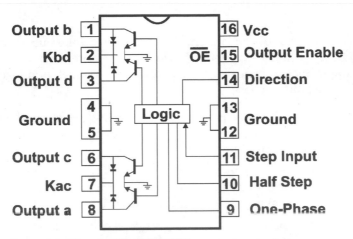

Figure 12.9   Pinout of the UCN 5804.

The schematic for a stepper motor controller using a dedicated IC is shown in Fig. 12.10, and a photograph of the circuit is shown in Fig. 12.11. The UCN 5804 is powered by a 5-V dc power supply. While it is internally powered by 5 V, it can control stepper motor voltages up to 35 V.

Notice in the schematic that there are two resistors, labeled rx and ry, that do not show any resistance value. Depending upon the stepper motor, these resistors may not be necessary. Their purpose is to limit current through the stepper motor to 1.25 A (if necessary).

Let's look at our 5-V stepper motor. It has a coil resistance of 13 Ω. The current draw of this motor will be 5 V/13 Ω = 0.385 A or 385 mA, well below the 1.25-A maximum rating of the UCN 5804. So in this case resistors rx and ry are not needed and may be eliminated from the schematic.

Before we move on, however, let's look at one more case, a 12-V stepper motor with a phase (coil) resistance of 6 Ω. The current drawn by this motor is 12 V/6 Ω = 2 A. This is above the maximum current rating of the UCN 5804. To use this stepper motor, you must add the rx and ry resistors. The rx and ry resistor values should be equal to each other, so that each phase will have the same torque. The values chosen for these resistors should limit the current drawn to 1.25 A or less. In this case, the resistors should be at least 4 Ω (5 to 10 W). With the resistors in place, the current drawn is 12 V/10 Ω= 1.20 A.

The inputs to the UCN 5804 are compatible with CMOS and TTL, meaning that we can connect the outputs from our PIC microcontroller directly to the UCN 5804 and expect it to function properly. The step input (pin 11) to the UCN 5804 is generated by the PIC microcontroller. The Output Enable pin enables the stepper motor when held low and disables (stops) the stepper motor when brought high (see Fig. 12.10).

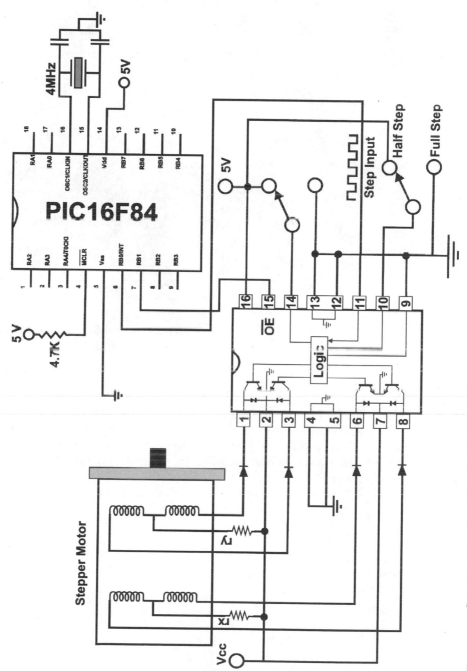

Figure 12.10 Stepper motor schematic using the UCN 5804.

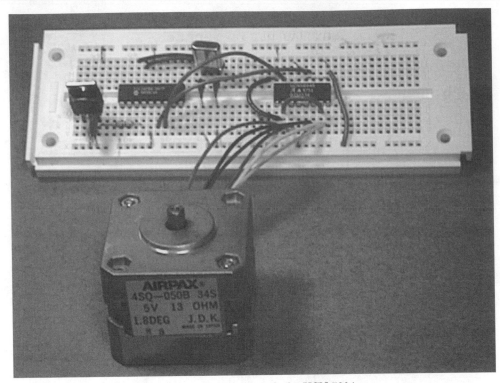

Figure 12.11   Photograph of stepper motor circuit with the UCN 5804.

Pins 10 and 14 on the UCN 5804 are controlled by switches that bring the pins to a logic high or low. Pin 10 controls whether the output to the stepper motor will be full-step or half-step, and pin 14 controls direction. If we want, these options may also be put under the control of the PIC. The pins are brought to logic high and low to activate the options in the same way as the Output Enable pin was activated.

The following is a PICBasic program that uses a dedicated stepper motor IC.

```
'Stepper motor w/ UCN 5804
Symbol TRISB = 134          'Initialize TRISB to 134
Symbol PortB = 6            'Initialize variable PortB to 6
Poke TRISB,0                'Set PortB lines output
Low1                        'Bring Output Enable low to run
start:
Pulsout 0, 10000            'Send 10-ms pulse to UCN 5804
Goto start                  'Do it again
```

In this case, I again wrote a simple core program to show how easily you can get the stepper motor running. You can, of course, add options to the program to change the pulse frequency, connect the direction and step mode pins, etc.

Parts List

(1) UCN 5804	Stepper motor controller chip
(1) 5 V	Stepper motor, unipolar (six-wire)
(1) 115 V/5 V	Stepdown wall transformer
(6)	1N914 diodes
(1)	TIP120 NPN transistors
(1)	7805 voltage regulator
(1)	Rectifier, 50-V, 1-A
(1)	150-μF capacitor
(1)	4050 hex buffer chip

Available from: Images Company, James Electronics, JDR MicroDevices, and RadioShack (see Suppliers Index).

Servomotor Control

Servomotors (see Fig. 13.1), are used in most radio-controlled model airplanes and expensive model cars, boats, and helicopters. Because of this hobbyist market, servomotors are readily available in a number of stock sizes. Servomotors have many applications in animatronics, robotics, and positioning control systems.

Fundamentally, servomotors are geared dc motors with a positional feedback control that allows the rotor to be positioned accurately. The specifications state that the shaft can be positioned through a minimum of 90° (±45°). In reality, we can extend this range closer to 180° (±90°) by adjusting the positional control signal.

There are three wire leads to a servomotor. Two leads are for power, +5 V and GND. The third lead feeds a position control signal to the motor. The position control signal is a single variable-width pulse. The pulse can be varied from 1 to 2 ms. The width of the pulse controls the position of the servomotor shaft.

A 1-ms pulse rotates the shaft to the extreme counterclockwise (CCW) position (−45°). A 1.5-ms pulse places the shaft in a neutral midpoint position (0°). A 2-ms pulse rotates the shaft to the extreme clockwise (CW) position (+45°).

The pulse width is sent to the servomotor approximately 50 times a second (50 Hz). Figure 13.2 illustrates the relationship of pulse width to servomotor position.

The first program sweeps the servomotor back and forth like a radar antenna. The schematic is shown in Fig. 13.3. I'm purposely keeping the program small in order to illustrate the core programming needed. A picture of this project is shown in Fig. 13.4.

The variable B3 holds the pulse-width value. Suppose we examine the Pulsout command

```
Pulsout Pin, Period
```

Pin, of course, is the pinout. The number used in *Period* is specified in 10-μs (microsecond) units. In the program, we are starting with B3 equaling 100, or

Figure 13.1   Picture of hobby 4- to 6-sV (42-oz torque) servomotors.

100×10 μs = 1000 μs or 1 ms. If we look back at our servo specifications, we see that a 1-ms pulse rotates the servo's arm to its leftmost position.

The program continues to smoothly increment the B3 variable, sweeping the servomotor's arm to its rightmost position at B3 = 200 (2 ms). At this point, the process reverses, and B3 begins to decrement back to 100.

This sweeping back and forth continues for as long as the program is run.

```
'Servo motor program
'Sweep left to right like a radar antenna
b3 = 100                              'Initialize at left position
sweep:
Pulsout 0,b3                          'Send signal to servomotor
Pause 18                              'Transmit signal 50-60 Hz
b3 = b3 + 1                           'Increment servo pulse width
If b3 > 200 Then sweepback            'End of forward sweep?
Goto sweep                            'Keep sweeping
sweepback:
b3 = b3 - 1                           'Decrement servo pulse width
Pulsout 0, b3                         'Send pulse to servomotor
Pause 18                              'Send it 50-60 Hz
If b3 < 100 Then sweep                'End of sweepback?
Goto sweepback                        'Keep going back
```

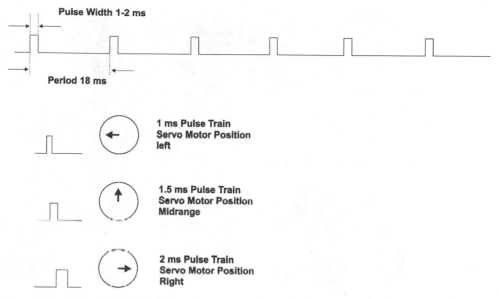

Figure 13.2 Pulse-width train delivered to servomotor. Relationship of pulse width to servomotor armature position.

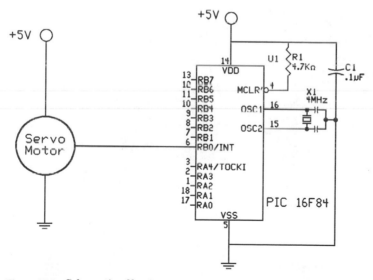

Figure 13.3 Schematic of basic servomotor sweeper controller (automatic).

Extending Servomotor Range

A pulse-width variance from 1 to 2 ms will provide a full 90° of rotation. To extend this range up to 180°, you need to use pulses smaller than 1 ms and greater than 2 ms.

If you decide to extend the rotational movement from your servo, you should be aware of certain problems that may arise. In particular, the servomotor has

Figure 13.4 Picture of automatic servomotor sweeper.

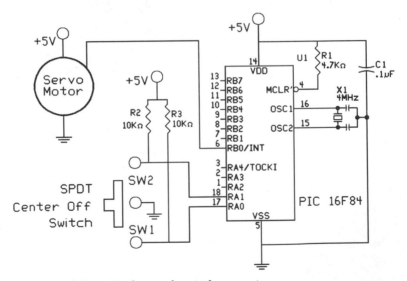

Figure 13.5 Schematic of manual control servomotor.

end stops that limit how far the shaft can rotate in either direction. If the PIC is sending a signal to the servomotor that is past either end stop, the motor will continue to fight against the end stop. In this stalled condition, the servomotor will draw increased current and generate greater wear on the gearing inside the motor, neither of which is desirable.

There is a within-group variance among servomotors from the same manufacturer as well as a variance among servomotor manufacturers. So while one servo may need a 2.8-ms pulse for a full rotation extension, another may require only a 2.4-ms pulse width.

When you decide to go out of the prescribed range of acceptable pulse widths (1 to 2 ms) for servomotors, you should check the individual servomotor to ensure that you are not stalling.

Manual Servo Control

This next project allows you to control the servomotor via a few switches. The schematic is shown in Fig. 13.5. The switch used is a single-pole, double-throw (SPDT) with a center off position. The center off position is essential. If there is not a center off position, you will need to use two switches instead of one.

The operation of this switch is simple. To activate the servo, move the switch in the upward direction. The servo will begin to rotate in one direction. To stop the motor, move the switch to the center off position. To rotate the servo in the opposite direction, push the switch lever down. Stop the servo as before, by placing the switch in the center off position. The complete project is shown in Fig. 13.6.

```
'Manual servo controller
Symbol porta = 5
b3 = 150                    'Initialize servo at center position
start:
Peek porta,b0               'Look at switches on port A
If bit0 = 0 Then sweep1     'Is SW1 pressed?
If bit1 = 0 Then sweepr     'Is SW2 pressed?
Pulsout 0,b3                'Hold servo in current position
Pause 18                    'Send signal 50-60 Hz
Goto start                  'Check switches again
sweep1:                     'SW1 is pressed
b3 = b3 + 1                 'Increment servo pulse width
Pulsout 0,b3                'Send signal to servo motor
```

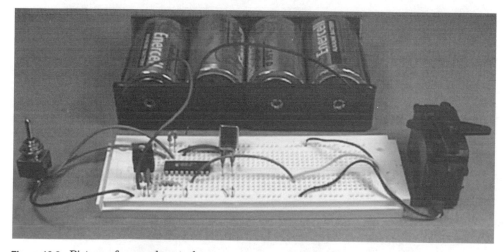

Figure 13.6 Picture of manual control servomotor.

```
Pause 18                         'Transmit signal 50-60 Hz
If b3 > 200 Then hold1           'Maximum sweepl value?
Goto start                       'Keep sweeping
sweepr:                          'SW2 is pressed
b3 = b3 - 1                      'Decrement servo pulse width
Pulsout 0, b3                    'Send pulse to servomotor
Pause 18                         'Send it 50-60 Hz
If b3 < 100 Then hold2           'Minimum sweepr value?
Goto start                       'Keep going back
hold1:                           'Hold maximum value to 200
b3 = 200
Goto start
hold2:                           'Hold minimum value to 100
b3 = 100
Goto start
```

Multiple Servomotors

Using the routines in the last servomotor program, you can easily connect three servomotors to the PIC 16F84 and still have four open I/O lines available for other duties.

The next project provides manual control for multiple (two) servomotors. It uses the core programming routines from the previous example.

The schematic adds a switch and a servomotor (see Fig. 13.7).

```
'Multiple servo controller program
Symbol porta = 5
b3 = 150                         'Initialize servo 1 at center position
b4 = 150                         'Initialize servo 2 at center position
start:
Peek porta,b0                    'Look at switches on port A
If bit0 = 0 Then sweepl          'Is SW1 pressed?
If bit1 = 0 Then sweepr          'Is SW2 pressed?
If bit2 = 0 Then sweepl2         'Is SW3 pressed?
If bit3 = 0 Then sweepr2         'Is SW4 pressed?
Pulsout 0,b3                     'Hold servo 1 in current position
Pulsout 1, b4                    'Hold servo 2 in current position
Pause 18                         'Send signal 50-60 Hz
Goto start                       'Check switches again
sweepl:                          'SW1 is pressed
b3 = b3 + 1                      'Increment servo pulse width
Pulsout 0,b3                     'Send signal to servo 1 motor
Pulsout 1, b4                    'Hold servo 2 position
Pause 18                         'Transmit signal 50-60 Hz
If b3 > 200 Then hold1           'Maximum sweepl value?
Goto start                       'Keep sweeping
sweepr:                          'SW2 is pressed
b3 = b3 - 1                      'Decrement servo pulse width
Pulsout 0, b3                    'Send pulse to servomotor
Pulsout 1, b4                    'Hold servo 2 position
Pause 18                         'Send it 50-60 Hz
If b3 < 100 Then hold2           'Minimum sweepr value?
Goto start                       'Keep going back
hold1:                           'Hold maximum value to 200
b3 = 200
Goto start
hold2:                           'Hold minimum value to 100
b3 = 100
```

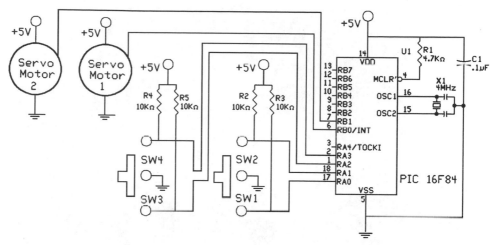

Figure 13.7   Schematic of multiple servomotor controller (manual).

```
Goto start
'Second servomotor routine
sweepl2:                        'SW3 is pressed
b4 = b4 + 1                     'Increment servo pulse width
Pulsout 1,b4                    'Send signal to servo 2 motor
Pulsout 0, b3                   'Hold servo 1 position
Pause 18                        'Transmit signal 50-60 Hz
If b4 > 200 Then hold3          'Maximum sweepl value?
Goto start                      'Keep sweeping
sweepr2:                        'SW4 is pressed
b4 = b4 - 1                     'Decrement servo pulse width
Pulsout 1, b4                   'Send pulse to servo 2 motor
Pulsout 0, b3                   'Hold servo 1 position
Pause 18                        'Send it 50-60 Hz
If b4 < 100 Then hold4          'Minimum sweepr value?
Goto start                      'Keep going back
hold3:                          'Hold maximum value to 200
b4 = 200
Goto start
hold4:                          'Hold minimum value to 100
b4 = 100
Goto start
```

The completed project is shown in Fig. 13.8.

Timing and Servomotors

As you experiment with servomotors, it is necessary to feed the pulse signal to the servomotor 50 to 60 times per second. It is important to keep this in mind when running multiple servomotors or other time-critical applications.

Parts List

Same components as in Chap. 1.

Figure 13.8 Picture of multiple manual servomotor controller.

Additional components

For each servomotor:

(1) Servomotor, 4–6 V, HS 300 (42-oz torque) or equivalent

(1) SPDT toggle switch with center off position

(2) 10-kΩ $\frac{1}{4}$-W resistors

Available from: Images Company, James Electronics, JDR MicroDevices, and RadioShack (see Suppliers Index).

Analog-to-Digital (A/D) Converters

Analog-to-digital (A/D) converters read an analog voltage and convert it into a digital equivalent number that can be read by a computer or microcontroller. Most phenomena in the real world are analog: intensity of light, sound, temperature, pressure, time, gravity, etc.

Analog Signal

Any analog signal, regardless of its origin, is infinitely variable between any two points. This holds true no matter how close those two points are. For instance, the number of possible volt readings between 1 V and 2 V is infinite. Some possible values are 1.1 V, 1.0000001 V, and 1.00000000000000000001 V. As you can see, voltage can vary by infinitesimal amounts.

Digital Equivalents

A digital equivalent of an analog signal is not infinitely variable. The digital equivalent changes in discrete, predefined steps. Figure 14.1 illustrates an analog signal and a digital equivalent. A rising voltage (analog signal) plotted digitally against time would jump in increments in a staircase-like fashion. Each step in the staircase represents a predetermined change in voltage, up or down, based upon the resolution and threshold of the A/D converter.

We can also observe from this drawing that the digital equivalents are updated only once per clock cycle. Complete clock cycles are indicated on the drawing as vertical tick marks. Therefore, in between complete clock cycles, no (digital) change is possible. The rise and fall of the digital equivalent signal change must be equal to a multiple of the A/D converter's resolution, indicated on the drawing as horizontal tick marks.

A/D Converters

There are a number of PIC microcontrollers with built-in A/D converters. Since we have done all our work with the PIC 16F84, I will continue to work with this chip by connecting an external A/D converter.

My next book, on PIC microcontrollers, will deal with more advanced PIC microcontrollers with built-in A/D converters.

To minimize the number of I/O lines needed, we will use a serial A/D converter. The TLC 548 is shown in Fig. 14.2. This serial A/D chip will require just three lines off our PIC microcontroller. The specifications on this A/D converter are as follows:

CMOS technology

8-bit resolution

Reference input voltages (±)

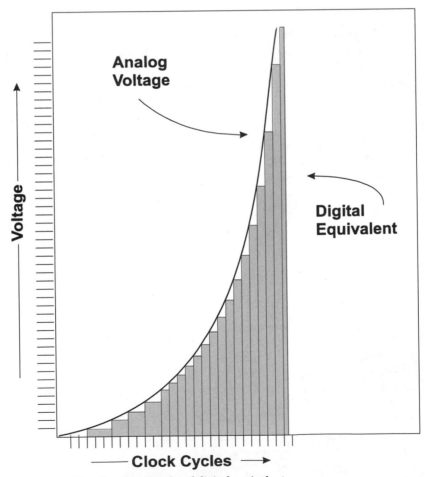

Figure 14.1 Plot of analog signal and digital equivalent.

Conversion time, 17 μs max

40,000 samples per second (approx.)

Built-in sample and hold

Wide power supply range, 3 to 6 V

4-MHz internal clock

Low power consumption, 6 mW (typical)

This chip is easily interfaced to our microcontroller.

Setting the Reference Voltage

Looking at the pinout of the integrated circuit shown in Fig. 14.2, we can see that there are two pins for setting the reference voltages, REF+ (pin 1) and REF− (pin 3). The voltages placed between these two pins become the range of voltages the analog-to-digital converter will read and convert to a digital equivalent.

The voltage difference between these two reference (REF) pins must be at least 1 V. REF+ should not be greater than the + power supply to the chip (V_{cc}). Consequently, REF− should not be less than the GND supply to the chip.

If desired, the REF+ pin can be tied to V_{cc} and the REF− pin can be tied to GND. This will allow the chip to read voltages between GND and V_{cc}.

Voltage Range and Resolution

Assuming a V_{cc} of +5 V, with REF+ tied to V_{cc} and REF− tied to ground, what is the resolution of our converter chip? We take our voltage range from REF− to REF+, in this case 5 V, and divide by our 8-bit resolution (or 256), which equals 5 V/256 = 0.019 V.

Looking back at Fig. 14.1, we could visualize each upward voltage increment (tick mark on vertical axis) as equaling 0.019 V.

Suppose the sensor or unit from which we need to read a voltage varies by only 2 V, say from 1 to 3 V. If we wanted to increase the resolution of our A/D

Top View

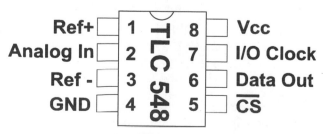

Figure 14.2 Pinout of the TLC 548.

converter, we could set REF− to 1 V and REF+ to 3 V. Now what is the resolution of our A/D converter? It's calculated just as before. We take the voltage range from REF− to REF+, in this case 2 V, and divide by 256 (8-bit resolution). So 2/256 = 0.0078 V.

Interpreting the Results

Suppose the PIC microcontroller is reading the number 100 from the serial A/D converter. What does this number represent? Let's go back to our first case, where V_{cc} is 5 V, the voltage range is 5 V, REF+ is tied to V_{cc}, and REF− is tied to ground. Our resolution is 0.019 V. So reading 100 from the A/D chip means that it is reading a voltage of 100×0.019 V, or 1.9 V.

In the second case, where REF− is at 1 V, REF+ is a +3 V, range equals 2 V, and step resolution equals 0.0078 V. Here reading the number 100 from the serial A/D converter is equal to a voltage of 1.78 V [$(100 \times 0.0078$ V $= 0.78$ V); 0.78 V plus REF− (1 V) = 1.78 V].

Serial Chip Control

Now that the basic calculations are finished, it's time to actually implement the chip. We need three I/O lines to use the serial A/D chip. The CS pin is a Chip Select; the small line or bar above the CS nomenclature tells us that the pin is active negative. Thus, when the CS pin is brought low, the chip is selected. A clock signal is sent to the chip's I/O clock pin. We read the serial data from the data out pin.

We will have to create our own serial routine as before, since the RS-232 communication protocol will foul the chip with its stop and start bits. But we will use the RS-232 routine to display the information from our A/D onto our LCD display.

Serial Chip Sequence

This sequence shows how the serial A/D chip can be accessed easily.

1. Bring the CS pin low. This immediately places the most significant bit (MSB) on the data out pin.
2. The falling edges of the first four I/O clock cycles shift out the second, third, fourth, and fifth most significant bits. At this point, the on-chip sample and hold begin sampling the analog input.
3. Three more I/O clock cycles bring out the sixth, seventh, and eighth conversion bits on the falling edges.
4. Bring CS high and the I/O clock line low.

The first schematic is shown in Fig. 14.3. We are using a 5- or 10-kΩ potentiometer. By moving the wiper back and forth, you can see how the number on the LCD changes. You can calculate the voltage the number represents by multiplying the number on the display by 0.019 V.

```
'Serial A/D converter program
Low 1                        'Bring I/O clock low
start:
Gosub serial_in
' LCD routine
Serout 3, N2400, (254, 1)
Pause 1
Serout 3, N2400, (#b0)
Pause 100                    'Let me see display
Goto start
'Serial in routine
serial_in:
Low 2                        'Bring CS down low
bit7 = pin0                  'Load bit 7 into B0
Pulsout 1,1                  'Bring CLK pin high, then low
bit6 = pin0                  'Load bit 6 into B0
Pulsout 1,1                  'Bring CLK pin high, then low
bit5 = pin0                  'Load bit 5 into B0
Pulsout 1,1                  'Bring CLK pin high, then low
bit4 = pin0                  'Load bit 4 into B0
Pulsout 1,1                  'Bring CLK pin high, then low
bit3 = pin0                  'Load bit 3 into B0
Pulsout 1,1                  'Bring CLK pin high, then low
bit2 = pin0                  'Load bit 2 into B0
Pulsout 1,1                  'Bring CLK pin high, then low
bit1 = pin0                  'Load bit 1 into B0
Pulsout 1,1                  'Bring CLK pin high, then low
bit0 = pin0                  'Load bit 0 into B0
Pulsout 1,1
High 2                       'Bring CS high
Return
```

Toxic Gas Sensor

A toxic gas sensor responds to a large number of airborne compounds (see Fig. 14.4). It is a resistive device; when it detects airborne compounds, its resistance

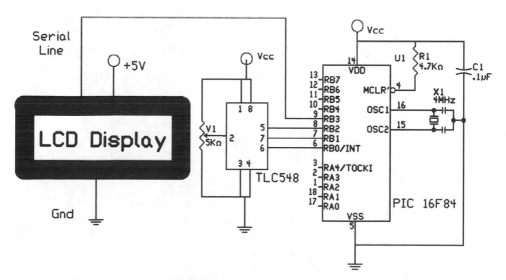

Figure 14.3   Test circuit using a 10-kΩ potentiometer.

decreases. Figure 14.5 is a schematic of the toxic gas sensor project. Pins 2 and 5 on the gas sensor are connected to an internal heater coil. The heater draws 115 mA at 5 V. Pins 4 and 6 are connected together internally, as are pins 1 and 3. You can solder wires to the sensor directly or purchase a round six-pin socket.

Polarity isn't important to the heater coil or resistive element. You may notice that as the sensor is operating, it will feel quite warm. Don't be alarmed; this is normal.

Since the sensor has been in storage prior to your receiving it, it will require an initial 2-min warm-up period when it is first turned on. The length of the warm-up period will decrease with repeated use. After the warm-up period, you can test the sensor with a number of household items.

For the first test, breathe on the sensor. The numbers on the LCD display should go up as it detects the carbon dioxide in your breath. For another test, release gas from a butane lighter. The sensor should react immediately to the butane gas.

Figure 14.6 is a photograph of the complete project.

In the next chapter, we will use this circuit to make a toxic gas alarm and automatic ventilator control.

Parts List

Same components as in Chap. 1.

Additional components

TLC548 Serial A/D $8.95
Toxic gas sensor $32.00
6-pin socket $1.50

Available from: Images Company (see Suppliers Index).

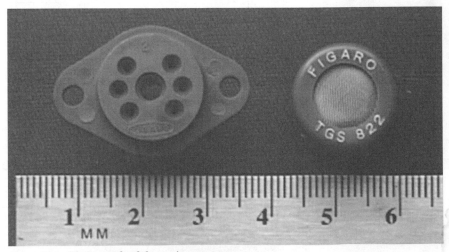

Figure 14.4 Photograph of the toxic gas sensor.

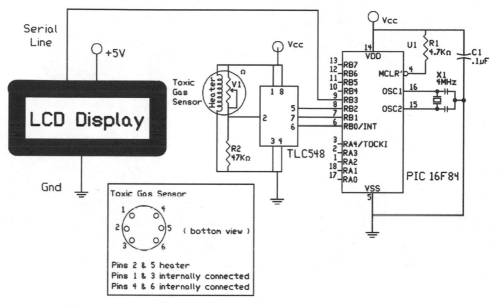

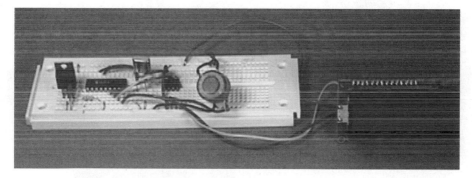

Figure 14.5 Schematic using toxic gas sensor.

Figure 14.6 Photograph of toxic gas sensor circuit.

Controlling AC Appliances

In our previous work, we connected the output of our PIC microcontrollers mostly to CMOS or TTL logic (+5 V) applications. What we will do in this chapter is use the PIC microcontroller output to control ac loads and appliances.

For our demonstration project, we will take the toxic gas sensor from Chap. 14 and make an automatic ventilation control system. This project is for demonstration purposes only. The PIC chip senses the real-world environment and then controls a real-world function. It is NOT, under any circumstances, to be used in any commercial or private application as a toxic gas detector, controller, or ventilation control.

The project is simple: When the PIC microcontroller senses a toxic gas, it will turn on an electric fan and keep it on until the gas concentration returns to a safe level.

Before we build our project, we will provide some useful information that you will need when designing an ac control system for yourself.

Inductive and Resistive Loads

Any device we power or control may be called a load. Whatever the electrical device (or load) may be, it will fall into one of two electrical categories, inductive or resistive. The type of device the load is will determine the type of circuit used to power and control it.

It's pretty easy to distinguish an inductive load from a resistive load. An inductive device (load) has wire coils and windings in it; examples are motors, transformers, relays, and solenoids. A resistive device doesn't have any inductive coils or wire windings; examples are incandescent lights, toasters, coffee makers, and heaters.

To control ac loads, we will use an optocoupler triac. The MOC 3010 is an optocoupler triac that is packaged as a six-pin DIP chip (see Fig. 15.1). When the PIC outputs a high signal (+5 V) on one of its I/O pins, connected to pin 1 on the MOC 3010, it will turn on an internal LED. The internal LED triggers a photosensitive internal triac (pins 6 and 4), which in turn will trigger an external triac that powers the load.

Circuit Construction

To build these circuits, you *cannot* safely use the solderless breadboard. The voltages and currents are greater than can be safely handled on the breadboard.

Please be careful. I don't want people accidentally shocking or electrocuting themselves. Always be extra careful when building any circuit that uses household electric power. The power available from your household electric wiring is more than enough to reduce your circuit to a cinder or to give you a nasty shock or worse.

Figure 15.2 shows a resistive-type ac appliance circuit fragment (minus the PIC controller). An inductive appliance controller is shown in Figure 15.3 (again minus the PIC microcontroller). The resistor R_L (in each schematic) is your main load or appliance that is being powered. The triac chosen will determine the maximum power (in watts) that may be safely controlled. The power rating on the triac I used (see Parts List) is 6 A at 200 V, more than enough for a 50-W fan.

I advise constructing the inductive-type circuit, since it can be used for both resistive and inductive types of appliances. This will eliminate any potential questions later on, such as, Is this a resistive or an inductive control circuit?

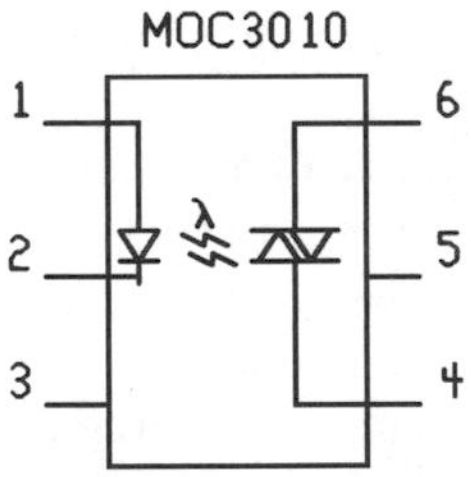

Figure 15.1 MOC3010 pinout.

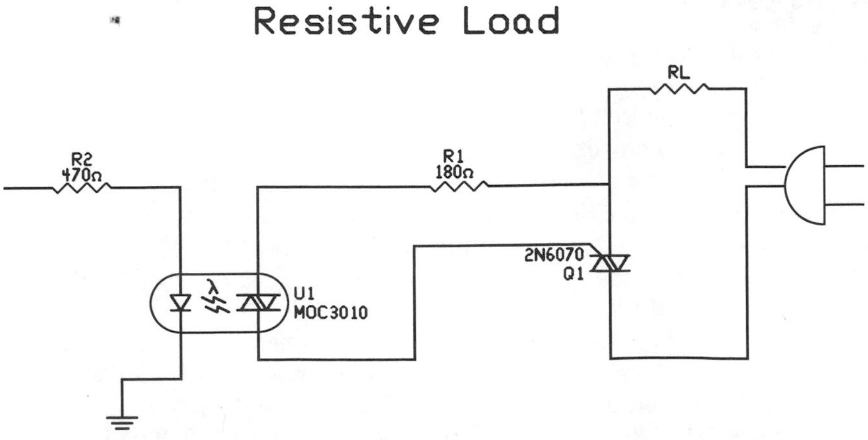

Figure 15.2 Resistive ac appliance circuit fragment.

Inductive Load

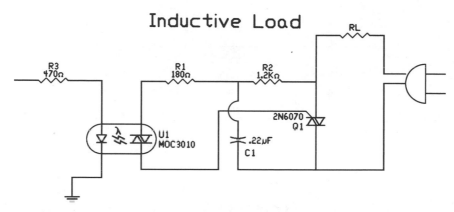

Figure 15.3 Inductive ac appliance circuit fragment.

The schematic fragment for resistive loads can be used for comparison with the inductive circuit or, if you wish, as a dedicated resistive load controller.

Since I believe that most readers will be interested in controlling ac appliances or devices in their home, Fig. 15.4 is the circuit we will build. All the components must be soldered to a printed circuit board. Make sure that any lines and wiring carrying the household power are adequately insulated and covered.

The triac l used is rated at 200 V at 6 A, which means that it is capable of handling 1200 W. In order to pass that much current, the triac would require an adequate heat sink. I advise you to keep the maximum power under 250 W.

```
'Serial A/D converter and toxic gas program
Low 1                           'Bring I/O clock low
start:
Gosub serial_in
' LCD routine
Serout 3, N2400, (254, 1)
Pause 1
Serout 3, N2400, (#b0)
Pause 100                       'Let me see display
If b0 > 190 Then fan1           'Turn fan on
If b0 < 191 Then fan2           'Turn fan off
Goto start
'Serial in routine
serial_in:
Low 2                           'Bring CS down low
bit7 = pin0                     'Load bit 7 into B0
Pulsout 1,1                     'Bring CLK pin high, then low
bit6 = pin0                     'Load bit 6 into B0
Pulsout 1,1                     'Bring CLK pin high, then low
Bit5 = pin0                     'Load bit 5 into B0
Pulsout 1,1                     'Bring CLK pin high, then low
bit4 = pin0                     'Load bit 4 into B0
Pulsout 1,1                     'Bring CLK pin high, then low
bit3 = pin0                     'Load bit 3 into B0
Pulsout 1,1                     'Bring CLK pin high, then low
bit2 = pin0                     'Load bit 2 into B0
Pulsout 1,1                     'Bring CLK pin high, then low
```

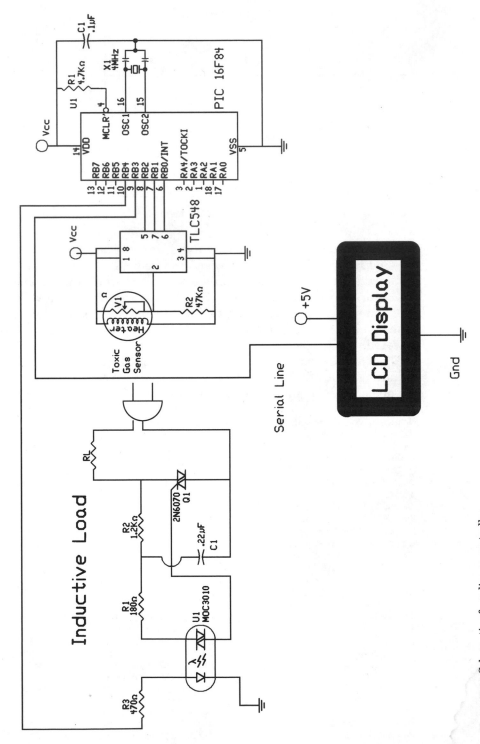

Figure 15.4 Schematic of appliance controller.

```
bit1 = pin0          'Load bit 1 into B0
Pulsout 1,1          'Bring CLK pin high, then low
bit0 = pin0          'Load bit 0 into B0
Pulsout 1,1
High 2               'Bring CS high
Return
fan1:
High 4
Goto start
fan2:
Low 4
Goto start
```

Test Circuit

If you want to test the program and circuit without building the entire circuit, you can. Remove the appliance power control section and replace it with a resistor and LED (see Fig. 15.5). When the microcontroller senses toxic gas, it turns on the LED. When the gas dissipates, the LED goes off.

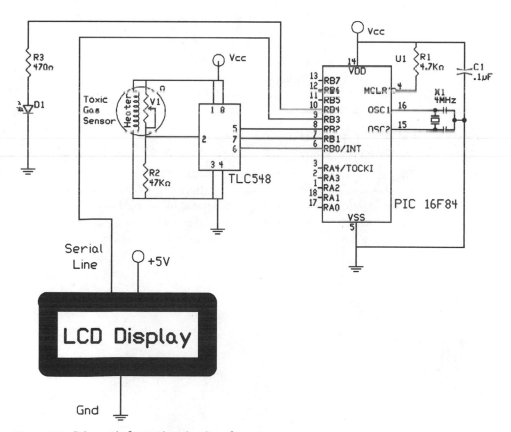

Figure 15.5 Schematic for testing circuit and program.

Smart Control

I would like to make a point regarding smart controls: They need feedback to determine if a particular action is being performed. To make this point, I wish to draw an analogy.

Let's say that you've just returned from a newspaper stand with your favorite magazine. You sit in a chair and reach over to turn on the lamp to read by, but there is no light. "Darn," you say to yourself. You look down to the socket to see if the lamp is plugged in. It is. You look over to the clock on the wall that's on the same fuse as the lamp. The clock is ticking away, so you know you have juice going to the lamp. You flick the lamp switch a couple of times, to make sure the switch isn't stuck. Now you take the lampshade off the lamp, and, sure enough, a black spot on the bulb lets you know that it's burned out. You replace the bulb, the lamp works fine, and you finally get to read the magazine.

Now, there's nothing remarkable about this incident. But it is a good example of a smart control. When the lamp was turned on, the person knew that the light wasn't lit and went through various steps to locate and correct the problem. But what about a microcontroller? Had it been the microcontroller's job to turn on the lamp, it would not have known whether the light was on.

To build a smart control, we must give the microcontroller feedback so that it can check to see if the action was successful. For the light example, we might use a photocell or photoresistor for a feedback signal. If the feedback gave a negative response, the microcontroller could ring an alarm or send a signal.

Keep this information in mind so that if someday you find that you have a need for a smart controller somewhere, your PIC chip can handle it.

Electronic Noses

The toxic gas sensor is the forerunner of the electronic nose. High-quality, highly selective electronic noses have numerous applications in many industries—food spoilage, perfume, medicine, and law enforcement, to name a few.

The toxic gas sensors are not digital sensors, they are analog. If there is sufficient within-group variance in the response to compounds, a group of sensors can be wired into a neural network for detection of specific odors.

Parts List

Same components as in Chaps. 1, 9, and 14.

Additional components

MOC3010 optocouple triac	RadioShack PN# 276-134
2N6070 triac (or equivalent)	RadioShack PN# 276-1000
0.22-μF capacitor	RadioShack PN# 272-1070
Line cord	RadioShack PN# 278-1255

470-Ω $\frac{1}{4}$-W resistor   RadioShack PN# 271-1317

180-Ω $\frac{1}{4}$-W resistor   RadioShack PN# RSU 11344702

1.2-kΩ $\frac{1}{4}$-W resistor   RadioShack PN# RSU 11344884

Miscellaneous components

Ac appliance small fan

Available from: Images Company, James Electronics, JDR MicroDevices, and RadioShack (see Suppliers Index).

Hexadecimal Numbers

The hexadecimal number system has a base of 16. It was found early on that base 16 (hexadecimal) is an ideal number system for working with digital computers. The reason this is so is that each nybble (4-bit number) is also base 16, so one hexadecimal digit can represent a 4-bit number.

As computer processors grew, they used larger and larger numbers. Regardless of how large these numbers become, they are, for the most part, evenly divisible by 4 bits. Early personal computers were 8-bit, then came 16-bit processors. Current personal computers are 32-bit. Future computers will be 64-bit, then 128-bit, and so on.

The PICMicro chips do not follow this convention. Instead, they use an odd number of bits throughout their internal structure (see Fig. 6.6).

Decimal	Binary	Hexadecimal
0	0000	0
1	0001	1
2	0010	2
3	0011	3
4	0100	4
5	0101	5
6	0110	6
7	0111	7
8	1000	8
9	1001	9
10	1010	A
11	1011	B
12	1100	C
13	1101	D
14	1110	E
15	1111	F
16	00010000	10h

Notice that 10 in hex is equal to 16 in our standard base 10. Sometimes a lowercase h is placed behind the number to identify it as a hex number and not base 10. An 8-bit number can be represented by 2 hexadecimal digits. The hex number FF represents the maximum number 8 bits can hold, 255.

As with base 10, each number going toward the left is a multiple. For instance, 20 in base 10 is really 2 times 10. In hexadecimal, 20 is 2 times 16.

Many compilers and assemblers use hexadecimal numbers to program code. When examining code for the PIC microcontrollers, you will undoubtedly run across hexadecimal as well as binary numbers.

Program Answers

Chapter 3

```
'Program 3.1B
Symbol TRISB = 134       'Set TRISB to 134
Symbol PortB = 6         'Set variable PortB to 6
Symbol X = B0            'Initialize variable X
'Initialize port(s)
Poke TRISB,0             ' Set port B pins to output
loop:
For X = 0 to 255
Poke PortB, X            'Place X value at port to light LEDs
Pause 250               'Pause, or counting proceeds too fast to see
Next X                  'Next X value
Goto loop
'Program 3.2B
'Program binary progression counting
'Initialize variables
Symbol TRISB = 134   'Assign TRISB to 134
Symbol PortB = 6     'Assign variable PortB the decimal value of 6
'Initialize port(s)
Poke TRISB,0             ' Set port B pins to output
loop:
B0 = 1                  ' Set variable to 1 to start counting
B1 = 0                 ' Set variable to 0
B3 = 1
Poke PortB, B0          'Place B0 value at port to light LEDs
Pause 250              'Without pause, counting proceeds too fast to see
For B2 = 0 to 6
B1 = B0 * 2            'Calculate next binary progressive number
B0 = B1               'Set B0 to new value
B3 = B3 + B1          'New holding variable
Poke PortB, B3        'Place new value at port to light LEDs
Pause 250            'Without pause, counting proceeds too fast to see
Next B2              'Next loop value
Poke PortB,0         'Reset to 0
Pause 250
Goto loop
```

Chapter 4

```
'Program 4.1b
Symbol TRISB = 134       'Set TRISB
Symbol TRISA = 133       'Set TRISA
```

```
Symbol PortB = 6              'Initialize variable PortB to 6
Symbol PortA = 5              'Initialize variable PortA to 5
'Initialize port(s)
Poke TRISB,0                  'Set port B pins as output
Poke TRISA,1                  'Set pin 1 of port A as input
loop1:                        'Counting loop
For B2 = 0 to 255             '
Poke PortB, B2                'Place b0 value at port to light LEDs
Pause 250                     'Without pause, counting proceeds too fast to see
Peek PortA,B0                 'Peek SW1 status on port A
If bit0 = 0 Then loop2        'If closed, jump to loop2
Next B2                       'Next b0 value
Goto loop1                    'Repeat
loop2:                        'Noncounting loop
Poke PortB,0                  'Turn off all LEDs
Peek PortA,B0                 'Peek SW1 status on port A
If bit0 = 1 Then loop1        'If opened, jump back to loop1
Goto loop2                    'Repeat
```

Chapter 8

Simple

```
' Serial interface
Symbol TRISB = 134           'Assign TRISB to 134
Symbol PortB = 6             'Assign variable PortB the decimal value of 6
'Initialize port(s)
Poke TRISB,0                 'Set port B as output port
Low 2                        'Set Latch Enable low
start:
b0 = 160                     'Put number 160 (10100000) into b0
Gosub serial
Gosub display               'Output the number serially to 74164
Pause 1000                  'Wait 1 s
b0 = 255                    'Put number 255 (11111111) into b0
Gosub serial                'Output the number serially to 74164
Gosub display
Pause 1000                  'Wait 1 s
b0 = 0                      'Put number 0 (00000000) into b0
Gosub serial                'Output the number serially to 74164
Gosub display
Pause 1000                  'Wait 1 s
Goto start                  'Do it again
display:
Pulsout 2,1                 'Pulse Latch Enable high
Return
'Serial out routine
serial:
pin0 = bit7                 'Bring pin 0 high or low, depending upon bit
Pulsout 1, 1                'Bring CLK line high then low
pin0 = bit6                 'Same as above
Pulsout 1, 1                'Same as above
pin0 = bit5
Pulsout 1, 1
pin0 = bit4
Pulsout 1, 1
pin0 = bit3
Pulsout 1, 1
pin0 = bit2
Pulsout 1, 1
pin0 = bit1
Pulsout 1, 1
```

```
pin0 = bit0
Pulsout 1, 1
Low 1
Return
```

Not simple

```
'REM serial SPO256
Symbol TRISB = 134
Symbol portb = 6
Symbol porta = 5
'Initialize ports
Poke TRISB,128              ' Set RB7 as input, all others (RB0 to RB6) as
                             outputs
'Check line status         ' Could be switch or could be TTL logic signals
start:
Pause 200                  ' Give a human a chance to press a button(s)
Peek porta,b0              ' Read port A
If b0 = 0 Then three       'Check both lines first (normally b0 = 3)
If bit0 = 0 Then hello     'Check line 0/alternative command: If b0 = 2
If bit1 = 0 Then world     'Check line 1/alternative command: If b0 = 1
Goto start
'
'Say word hello
hello:                          'It's not just a word, it's a routine
For b3 = 0 to 5                 'Loop using number of allophones
Lookup b3,(27,7,45,15,53,1),b0 'Decimal addresses of allophones
Gosub speak                     'Speak subroutine
Next b3                         'Get next allophone
Goto start                      'Do it again from the beginning
'
'Say word world
world:                          'Procedure similar to hello
For b3 = 0 to 4
Lookup b3,(46,58,62,21,1),b0
Gosub speak
Next b3
Goto start
'
'Say sentence See you next Tuesday.
three:                              'Procedure similar to hello
For b3 = 0 to 19
Lookup b3,(55,55,19,1,49,22,1,11,7,42,55,13,2,13,31,43,2,33,20,1),b0
Gosub speak
Next b3
Goto start
'
speak:                     'Subroutine to speak allophones
pin0 = bit7                'Set up allophone address
Pulsout 1,1                'Pulse CLK line
pin0 = bit6
Pulsout 1,1
pin0 = bit5
Pulsout 1,1
pin0 = bit4
Pulsout 1,1
pin0 = bit3
Pulsout 1,1
pin0 = bit2
Pulsout 1,1
pin0 = bit1
```

```
Pulsout 1,1
pin0 = bit0
Pulsout 1,1
Low 6                      'Bring ALD low
Pause 1                    'Pause 1 ms for everything to latch
High 6                     'Bring ALD high
wait:
Peek portb,b0             'Look at port B
If bit7 = 0 Then wait     'Check SBY line (0 = talking, 1 = finished)
Return                    'Get next allophone
```

Suppliers Index

Images Company
39 Seneca Loop
Staten Island, NY 10314
(718) 698-8305
http://www.imagesco.com

James Electronics
1355 Shoreway Road
Belmont, CA 94002
(650) 592-8097
http://www.jameco.com

JDR Microdevices
1850 South 10 Street
San Jose, CA 95112-4108
(800) 538-5005
http://www.jdr.com

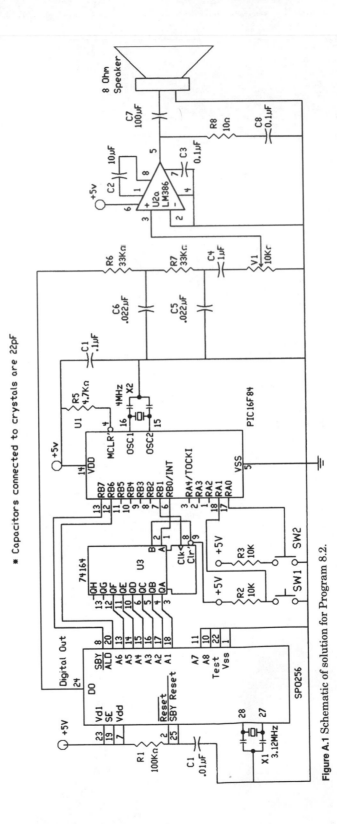

Figure A.1 Schematic of solution for Program 8.2.

ABOUT THE AUTHOR

John Iovine is the author of several popular TAB titles that explore the frontiers of scientific research. He wrote the cult classic *Robots, Androids, and Animatrons,* as well as *Homemade Holograms: The Complete Guide to Inexpensive, Do-it-Yourself Holography, Kirlian Photography: A Hands-On Guide; Fantastic Electronics: Build Your Own Negative-Ion Generator and Other Projects;* and *A Step into Virtual Reality.*